Kazuo Nishii

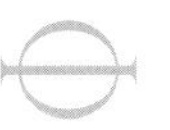

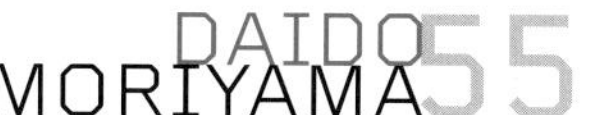

# DAIDO MORIYAMA 55

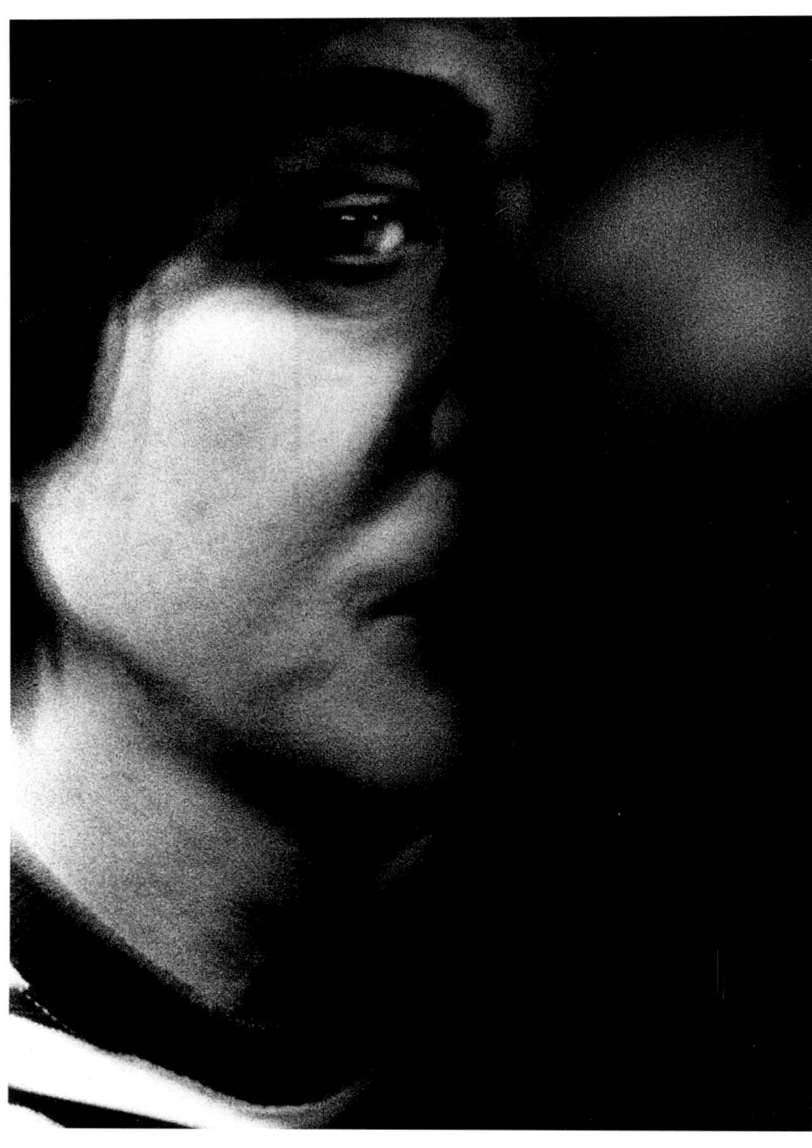

Self-portrait, 1997

2.3

Daido Moriyama is a radical and an innovator. When he emerged in the mid-1960s, photography was still widely considered to be an objective medium. One expected it to give a reliable account of external conditions, no matter how distinctive or subjective the photographer's point of view. Moriyama quickly broke with these unrealistic expectations. Almost from the outset, he also questioned what constitutes acceptable subject matter. All that can be grasped with any confidence, he seems to suggest, is what comes immediately to hand and eye: pictures in magazines, screen images and photographs constitute reality quite as much as actual objects. And while these images may, to most of us, signify a distant event, to Moriyama they are real enough to be photographed. He could only report on what came his way, and if it was prosaic, blurred or hastily glimpsed in passing, that provisional state of affairs was deemed acceptable. Much of the avant-garde photography of the 1980s and 1990s, Japanese, European and American, was influenced by his example. He established a tendency and even a style; but what sets him apart is that his sceptical approach is genuine, part of the predicament of an authentic outsider.

This sense of himself as an 'outsider' was largely attributable to the fact that Moriyama spent much of his childhood on the move, due to his father's profession as a travelling insurance salesman. Born and brought up for a while in Osaka, he returned to the city of his birth to study graphic design, going freelance as a designer in 1958. It was around this time that he also became interested in photography. There seem to have been no special circumstances or happy accidents involved in his entry into photography, but clearly he had found his way. He studied under Takeji Iwamiya in Osaka, and his early influences included William Klein's *Life is Good and Good for You in New York: Trance Witness Revels* (1956).

In 1961 Moriyama moved to Tokyo, hoping to join the VIVO group of photographers, which included Eikoh Hosoe and Shomei Tomatsu. VIVO was on the point of dissolving, but Moriyama was taken on as Hosoe's assistant and also got to know Tomatsu, who became a major influence. Going freelance in 1963, he began to establish himself the following year, when he met Takuma Nakahira, editor of an important leftist magazine, *The Modern Eye*, and the poet and dramatist Shuji Terayama. Another new acquaintance was Hideo Kinoshita, editor of *Asahi Graph*, which began, along with *Asahi Journal* and *Asahi Camera*, to publish his pictures.

In the early summer of 1965, Moriyama moved to Zushi, in Kanagawa Prefecture, just south of Tokyo and Yokohama, the same area to which Takuma Nakahira, who had recently taken up photography, had also moved. Whilst taking pictures at the nearby American naval base of Yokosuka, Moriyama began to work in what was to become his trademark snapshot style. Japan was witnessing the beginning of a long period of economic growth, initially boosted by the Tokyo Olympics of 1964. This was accompanied by a surge of mass culture, both in production and consumption, and commercial photography was flourishing. Advertising agencies were employing more and more photographers, and camera work became a star profession. Shoji Yamagishi, editor of the magazine *Camera Mainichi*, was deft at spotting talented young photographers, and offered many of them work. It was he who first published Moriyama's photographs of the Yokosuka naval base. 'Bring me any piece at any time and I'll put it in the magazine', he is reported to have said to the young photographer. In 1967 Moriyama's series of showmen appeared in four successive issues of *Camera Mainichi*, earning him the accolade of Most Promising Photographer, awarded by the Japan Photography Critics Association. This award established Moriyama in the public eye.

Moriyama's interest in showmen was stimulated by his connection with Shuji Terayama, then leader of the experimental theatre group Tenjyo-Sajiki. Their first collaboration had been in 1966 in the magazine *Haiku*, with a series called 'The Underpinnings of Show Biz: A Postwar History of Sideshows'. Moriyama's 'Showmen' series of the next year contained images of strolling players, traditional popular singers (such as Saburo Kitajima) and vaudeville performers from the lower-class Asakusa district of Tokyo. Critics praised the work for its insightful exploration of the 'Japanese vernacular' and the 'entertainments of common people'. But this was never Moriyama's aim; his photographs did not arise from an interest in popular entertainment per se. In 1968 he compiled *Japan: A Photo Theatre* (with an introductory text by Terayama), to articulate his discontent with the reception of his work. The photographs were wide-ranging in style and type, and were far from demonstrating an unproblematic display of enthusiasm for popular entertainment. As the title suggests, Moriyama felt that urban life had assumed the quality of a stage or film set. Urbanization was rife, and everywhere one turned, new shopping streets were appearing, often named in imitation of Tokyo's most fashionable commercial avenue, the Ginza. Regional cities were mimicking the centre with a rapidly growing, standardized sprawl.

In partnership with Terayama, Moriyama launched the magazine *Scandal* in late 1968. His preoccupation with this publication accounts for his absence from the roster in the first issue of *PROVOKE*, which was to prove a landmark in Japanese photography. *PROVOKE* was primarily a coterie magazine. It was published in a square format, 21 x 21 cm, and its launch issue was little more than a brochure of around seventy pages. Its all-black title page bore the word PROVOKE in English, printed in grey, followed by a text in smaller, white letters giving the Japanese transliteration and the subtitle 'Provocative Materials for Thinkers, quarterly, no. 1'. The contributors were aware of the signboard famously hung up outside Eugène Atget's atelier in 1892, 'Materials for Artists', when he gave up painting for photography. On the magazine's second page was a short text by the PROVOKE group; intended as their manifesto it reads: 'Words have lost the material force that once held reality, and they float freely now in air. At such a time, it is for photographers to capture with their eyes the remaining vestiges of reality that words can no longer reach. We feel we must present these provocative materials to the words themselves. We have given the subtitle "provocative materials for thinkers", despite some misgivings, to this end. Yutaka Takanashi, Takuma Nakahira*, Koji Taki*, Takahiko Okada (*Founders).'

In 1968 an international youth movement was contesting the status quo. A wave of protests, sit-ins and strikes took place in universities throughout the world, and these were especially severe in Japan, Tokyo and Nohon Universities being the two pillars of revolt. Nakahira was directly involved in these protests, and he also supported them off campus. He was seen by photography students as a core ideologue. The immediate occasion for the launch of *PROVOKE* was an important exhibition of photography, 'The 100 Year History of Japanese Photography', curated by Shomei Tomatsu. Nakahira and Koji Taki helped Tomatsu with this exhibition, but in the process they realized that they should try to assert an independent, alternative voice in the face of the authority embodied by Tomatsu. *PROVOKE* was their response, and although it only survived for three issues its influence, especially on a younger generation of photographers, was immense. As Moriyama's colleague Nobuyoshi Araki recalled: 'Most people paid no attention to it, but really it was like a bomb in Japanese photography.'

Classical documentary practitioners see the photograph as nothing more than a visual sign pointing to the existence of something else – the object in front of the camera. In these terms, a photograph merely proves that the object was once in a particular place, or that an action occurred at a certain time. To the members of PROVOKE, the real excitement and enigma of photography began at precisely this point. They were aware that photography cannot offer a complete record, and that it was this very partialness that led them to choose it as their medium of expression. The special kind of expressiveness they saw in the photograph was the way in which it could impart the experience of the moment. Time past is expunged in favour of a permanent present. The PROVOKE photographers viewed the act of pressing the shutter as affirmation of their 'own immediate reality, and no one else's'. Nakahira called this 'a desperate measure' to 'capture the inner aspect of our own life'.

The PROVOKE photographers not only pitted themselves against objective documentary work, but also contested the conventions of the well-taken or 'good' photograph, confined in its frame and enslaved to the aesthetics of composition. Instead, they extolled that which lay outside the frame. According to Nakahira, 'just one centimetre from photographed reality is another reality beyond your imagination'. Mis-shots were therefore considered authentic and equal to any other shot. Grainy, blurry pictures that would normally be discarded were deemed acceptable. Seeking the 'ideal' image, they caught images through blank triggering (when the shutter is depressed to move the film on after loading), and took 'no-finder' shots (where no reference is made to the viewfinder) and 'strobe-fired' shots (taken the moment a strobe, wielded by the photographer, blinds the eye). These truly conveyed a 'lived moment'.

When Nakahira invited Moriyama to join his group in time for the second issue of *PROVOKE* in November 1968, the latter contributed twenty-two pictures revealing the unfolding of his affair with a woman in what appears to be a 'love hotel'. These shots are out of focus, and maintain the woman's anonymity. Today, they still retain the sweaty immediacy of the moment they were shot.

Moriyama's contribution to the third and final issue of *PROVOKE* was a group of pictures taken at night in a supermarket called 'Yours on Aoyama Street'. Outside, demonstrators clashed with police; inside Moriyama made hurried, blurred pictures of the American goods stocked by the supermarket: Campbell's canned soup, tins of creamed Green Giant corn, crates of Coca-Cola and boxes of detergent. Andy Warhol's world was melodramatically rediscovered in the street-store where it had originated.

In 1969, Moriyama published the series 'Accident' in the monthly magazine *Asahi Camera*. The first set of the series, 'Images of a Certain Seven Days', consisted of reproductions from the media such as television, tabloid newspapers and magazines. One picture was appropriated from a road-safety poster showing a car crash. These rephotographed images were printed using high-key contrasts, their highlights sharply bleached, their shadow details blackened out into a continuous tone. Moriyama gave everything before his eyes – from cigarettes to matches to TV screens – 'equal epistemic or evidential value'. This, he said, was his 'governing policy'. He had already rephotographed published images in *Photo Theatre*, where he accepted no border between 'lived reality' and 'the reality of the image', even claiming that he sensed reality 'far more vividly' in a photographed woman than in a living one. He attributed this perverse discovery to the shock he felt on seeing pictures of Robert

F. Kennedy's assassination during the US presidential nominations. He had been overwhelmed by a feeling of strong reality while standing on a railway platform looking at the scattered newspaper 'extras' with their pictures of the dead senator. 'Images from a Certain Seven Days' was intended to shock, not by confounding the boundary between living reality and images, but by claiming that the virtualization of the living world had progressed so far that genuine reality could now only be found in a double removal, in 'reproductions of what are already reproduced images'. This multi-layering created a virtual image of a virtual image.

Moriyama's notion of 'equal epistemic or evidential value' gave rise to a theory of 'anonymity', which he, along with Nakahira and others, began to advance, introducing the term into their discourse on photography. Other photographers asked whether it was not a contradiction to assert such anonymity whilst presenting and signing these works as their 'own'. But Moriyama and friends saw the photographer's role as selecting the frame rather than simply pressing the shutter – which, according to Moriyama, meant by the same token that a picture of himself taken by someone else could also be considered 'his' photograph. The group proposed a 'distance' between the photographer and the subject, such that the photographer becomes the first viewer rather than the originating creator. The word 'distance' implies a psychological as well as a spatial remoteness; Moriyama and his associates were the first photographers to be conscious of this dual distance. Their concept of anonymity might have been prompted by the work that Nakahira and Taki had undertaken in 1968 for Shomei Tomatsu's '100 Year' show, when Nakahira announced that photography 'will amount to something only when it ceases to be an art striving for expression of an inner self, and begins to accept its documentary role'. He then began taking pictures with a studiedly objective attitude. Moriyama's notion that everything before his eyes had the same value and were documents rather than artistic expressions, surely stemmed from Nakahira's belief. He threw out a fundamental challenge to those who believed that photography could act as a vehicle for artistic self-expression by asking 'What is the photograph?', and 'Who is the photographer?'

When rephotographing from a printed original, the focus cannot be sharp or the 'dots' used in the initial printing process will appear. If an original is cheaply printed, as is often the case with tabloids and magazines, the definition will be low from the start, perhaps even too low to include much contrast. Rephotographed pictures must therefore be in high contrast. Thinking about such questions, Moriyama concluded that the spontaneous, accidental images found at the beginnings and ends of films, which always have extremely high contrast, were the most authentic photographs. Images unintentionally exposed on film ends were, after all, the epitome of anonymous pictures because they were the pure work of the machine called a camera and not of the photographer. Even streaking caused by accidental scratches on the film was, to him, acceptable.

The new, streaked, 'no-finder' photography was introduced to the public in 1970 in the only book published by PROVOKE, just before it was discontinued by Nakahira, *First Discard Likeness*. The photographs contributed by Moriyama to this publication resembled those that were to appear later in his *Farewell Photography* (1972). Moriyama really had jettisoned 'likeness', as the book's title enjoined. His photographs were extremely fuzzy and blurred, some so streaked and indistinct that it was impossible to make out even a trace of identifiable form, never mind verisimilitude, only varying shades and grains. Some prints were accidental exposures, some close-ups of cheap-print magazine pictures, revealing the dots.

Having pushed photography to such extremes, what was left for Moriyama to do? In *Memories of a Dog* (1984), he reflected on his response to *Farewell Photography*: 'Although I had intended to pursue the relationship between the watcher and the watched or that of taking photographs and presenting them, I suddenly came up against a brick wall. The publication did not leave me with a feeling of satisfaction; all that remained was irritation.'

Nineteen seventy-two was also the year of publication of *Hunter*, a book of more naturalistic pictures edited by Shoji Yamagishi and introduced by the graphic designer Tadanori Yokoo. Dedicated to Jack Kerouac, it is made up of 'road' pictures that report on Japanese culture and life. In his introduction, Yokoo claimed that Moriyama was an innately political photographer: 'Some photographers are apolitical, no matter how much they try to take a political stand, but he is just the opposite. The more he tries to avoid political themes, the more political his work seems to become.' Yokoo also commented that 'He takes his pictures from the point of view of a peeping Tom or a rapist ... Eyes that see from the windows of a moving car or from the shadows are those of a criminal. His pictures are like someone who talks, without looking people in the eye.' Finally, he remarked that Moriyama 'has no hometown – at least not the conventional physical sort. That must be why he wanders all over Japan taking pictures.' Moriyama had, in fact, been 'on the road' from 1969 to 1973, taking a long drive through Japan, very much in the style of Kerouac. He referred to his photographs of this period as 'abrasions' received as he scraped past society.

By 1970, Moriyama was well known in Japan. Throughout this entire year, *Asahi Camera* featured his work on its front cover. He also held a successful exhibition, 'Scandal', at Plaza Dick in Tokyo, made up of enlarged images of magazine adverts, and he often appeared on television and in advertisements. In late 1971, he went to New York with Yokoo, and whilst there, was impressed by the photography of Weegee, who offered a kind of retrospective endorsement for his own art – especially as it would appear in *Hunter* in 1972.

Nevertheless, Moriyama seems to have reached a hiatus around this time. *Farewell to Photography* was more than an arresting title. Aware of a creative falling off, he turned increasingly to alcohol and drugs, only emerging from this crisis in the early 1980s. During this fallow period, he never gave up completely. He turned in particular to the Japanese countryside for solace and inspiration, after more than a decade of immersion in the darker side of Japan's urban scene. In 1972, he visited historic sites and places of natural beauty, although he photographed them in the same brutally informal manner he had employed in the city. His 1974 series 'Cherry Blossoms', made for Camera Mainichi, was so strikingly gloomy that one reviewer was convinced Moriyama was on the verge of suicide.

In 1974, Moriyama extended his investigation of the essential Japan when he undertook a project based on *The Tales of Tono* (*Tono monogatori*), a series of folk-tales collected in 1910 by the ethnologist Kunio Yanagita in the northern village of Tono, which are now important elements in Japanese folklore. There are 119 of these tales, many of them gory, unsettling and fragmentary. Yukio Mishima, writing in 1970 just before his own suicide, described them as speaking 'coldly, of innumerable deaths'. Moriyama spent three days at

Tono photographing intensively. His new *Tales of Tono* were both published and exhibited in 1974, framed in pairs, almost as if they were stills from a disconnected narrative. Again, though he later described his motivation during the early 1970s, at the onset of his crisis, as 'wanting to get in touch with nature', these pictures look more as if he were trying to extend his dysfunctional urban aesthetic to the heartlands. He presents Tono as anything but an uplifting example of 'essential Japan'; instead, it is more like a countrified version of the disfigured urban landscapes on which he had focused in the 1960s.

Moriyama never changed his outlook, chose to go straight, or abjured his anarchic manner of the 1960s. Describing his art in his book *A Dialogue with Photography*, he wrote: 'I brush aside words and ideas, and focus on photography as a means of expressing a message that is both physiological and phenomenological. Without that framework, my approach is very simple – there is no artistry, I just shoot freely. For example, most of my snapshots I take from a moving car, or while running, without a finder, and in those instances one might say that I am taking the pictures more with my body than with my eyes. I think that the process gives my photos more a sense of place and existence, more atmosphere ... Whether it's the perception of a certain object, or the atmosphere of a situation, if one always thinks about the composition of the picture, one will lose the freshness of the moment, and little by little the photos reveal their contemplated and formatted nature ... [My] photos are often out of focus, rough, streaky, warped, etc. ... But if you think about it, a normal human being will in one day receive an infinite number of images, and some are focused upon, others are barely seen out of the corner of one's eye.'

In a long and revealing statement Moriyama goes on to conclude that for him: 'Photography is not the endeavour to create a two-dimensional work of art, but by taking photo after photo, I come closer to truth and reality at the very intersection of the fragmentary nature of the world and my own personal sense of time. To differentiate subjective and objective photography is nonsense.'

In 1982, after some years of abstention, Moriyama returned to photography with the book *Light and Shadow*, and on the death of his mother, returned to his birthplace to take pictures for the series, 'The Time of the Dog'. He had spent some time studying the work of Nakaji Yasui, the great amateur photographer of pre-war Japan, and Joseph Nicéphore Niépce, the French discoverer of the photographic process. In his book of 1990, *Lettre à Saint-Loup*, Moriyama makes reference to Niépce, whose country estate was at Saint-Loup-de-Varennes, near Chalon-sur-Saône. Using a camera obscura, Niépce, had taken an eight-hour exposure of the courtyard there. Moriyama claimed that the essence of his own memories and photography turned 'upon a certain spot in that scene of a summer day in Saint-Loup'.

With respect to Yasui, who took pictures of marginals and refugees, Moriyama remarked that one of photography's essential qualities is its amateurism, and another its anonymity. These have numbered among his aesthetic preoccupations almost from the beginning. On the one hand, there was the urge towards self-expression, which had to be resisted because it often depended on too great a degree both of self-awareness and of pictorial tradition. On the other, there was the banal objectivity of documentary photography. Somewhere between these poles lay photography proper, in which appearances somehow expressed themselves by means of the photographer as agent. This he achieved in the grip of the moment, working intensively as he did in Tono, or during the riots of the late 1960s, taking pictures from a moving car, or running through the night-world alleyways of the city.

Moriyama's given name, Hiromichi, means 'Great Road' (his twin brother, Kazumichi – 'Single Road' – died at the age of one). Writers and critics who have tried to give an account of Moriyama's work sometimes refer to his 'demons'. Perhaps these were born in those early days of his childhood, spent restlessly on the great road, and continued to plague him throughout his disturbing art. Whatever the truth of this, although his work has been much imitated, it remains as distinctive as the music of the great blues artists, which is perhaps how it might best be understood.

**Foetus, Kanagawa, Japan, 1966.** This picture on the theme of 'infancy' was taken at an old private maternity hospital with a long corridor of shelves loaded with glass cases. Inside were preserved foetuses in various stages of development. As a schoolboy, Moriyama had been startled to observe in his biology textbook the similarity between human, rabbit and turtle foetuses, a traumatic realization that would stay with him forever. The hospital director allowed him to photograph the foetus bottles in a makeshift studio set up in an unused operating theatre. He shot over three days, and six months later published the series, entitled 'Pantomime', in the monthly magazine *Modern Eye*

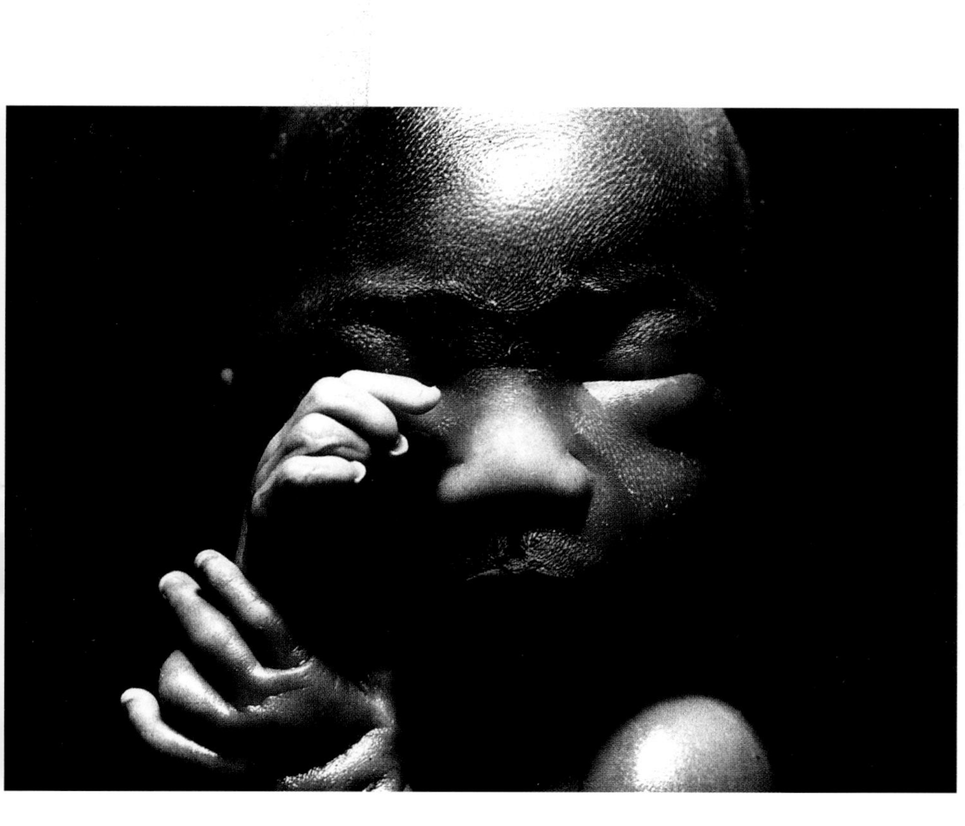

**Actor, Tokyo, Japan, 1966.** This image of a strolling female impersonator is from the series 'The Theatre of Japan', published in *Camera Mainichi*, January 1967. The series, depicting showmen, was later made into the book *Japan: A Photo Theatre* (1968). Moriyama has always been interested in issues of identity, in this instance, those connected with gender.

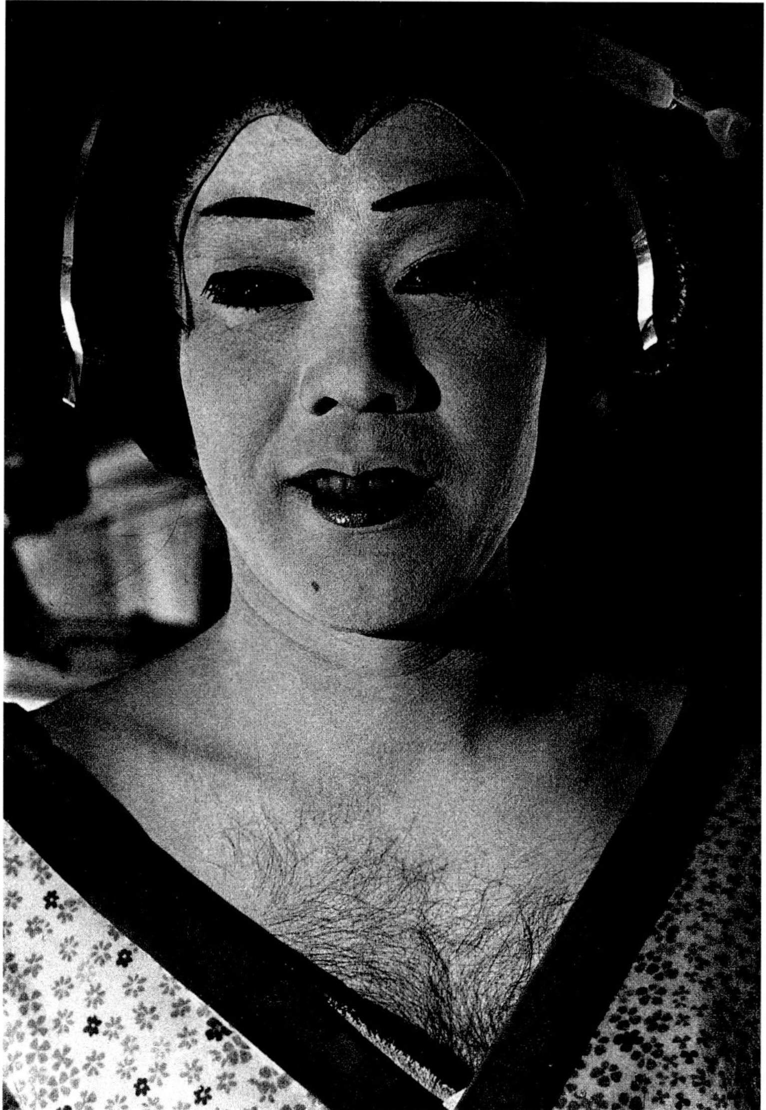

**Backstage, Tokyo, Japan, 1966.** This picture features another itinerant actor from 'The Theatre of Japan' series. His face, strongly sidelit, has a mask-like appearance; the figure to the left, just beginning to move out of frame, seems to have been decapitated. This is a brusquely masculine image with undertones of violence, in sharp contrast to the genial femininity of the figure in the previous image (page 19).

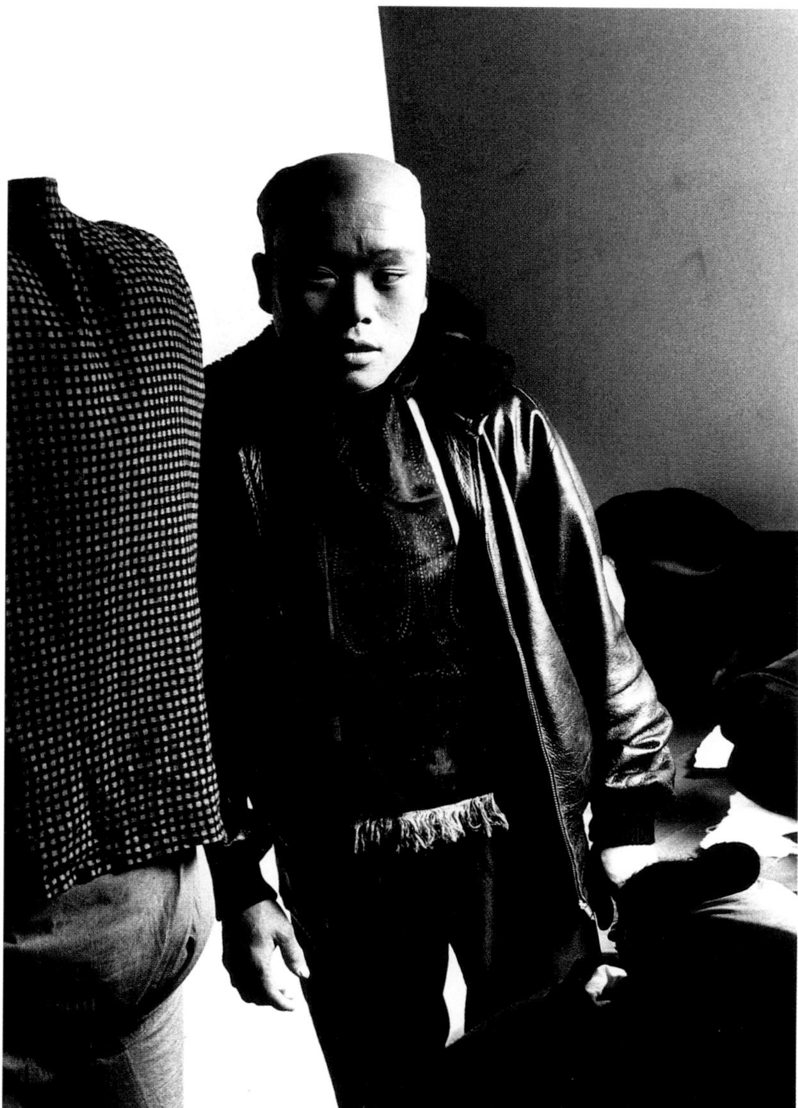

**Comedian, Tokyo, Japan, 1967.** This picture originally appeared in *Camera Mainichi*, May 1967, under the title *The Actor Shimizu Isamu*. Shimizu performed clownish skits in the breaks between theatre acts. His diminutive stature is indicated by his outsize shirt; the brush handle also gives a sense of scale. Perhaps he is laughing at the care Moriyama has taken with his staging.

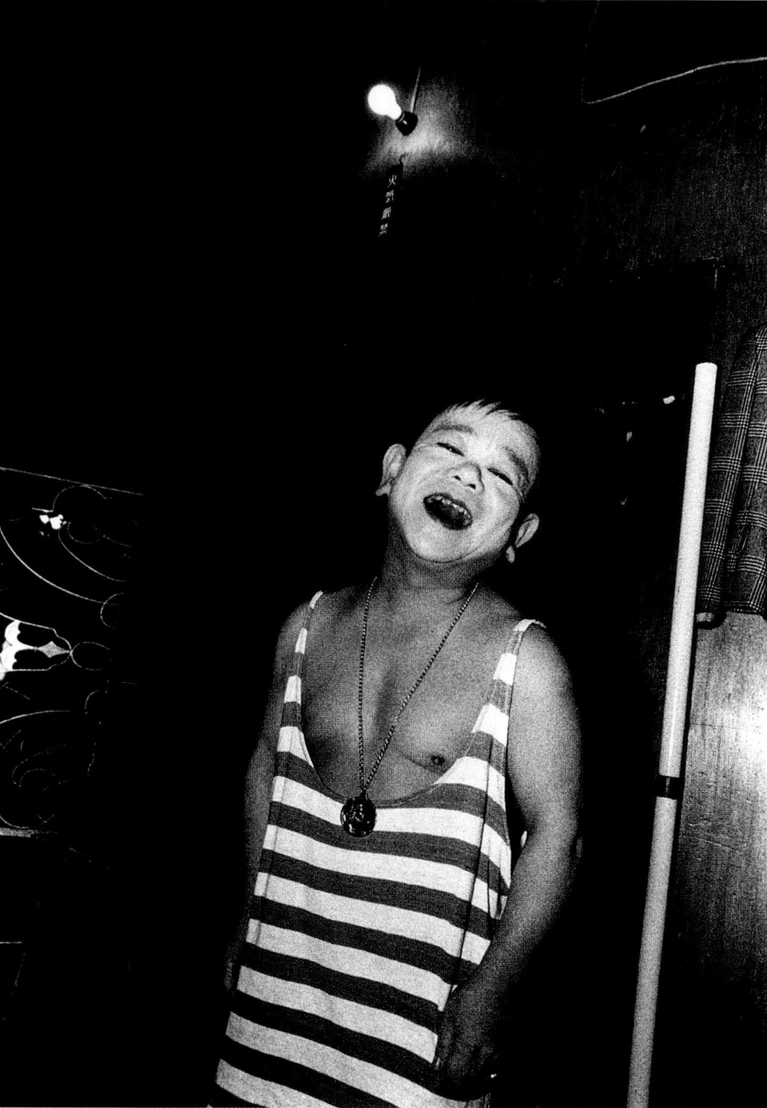

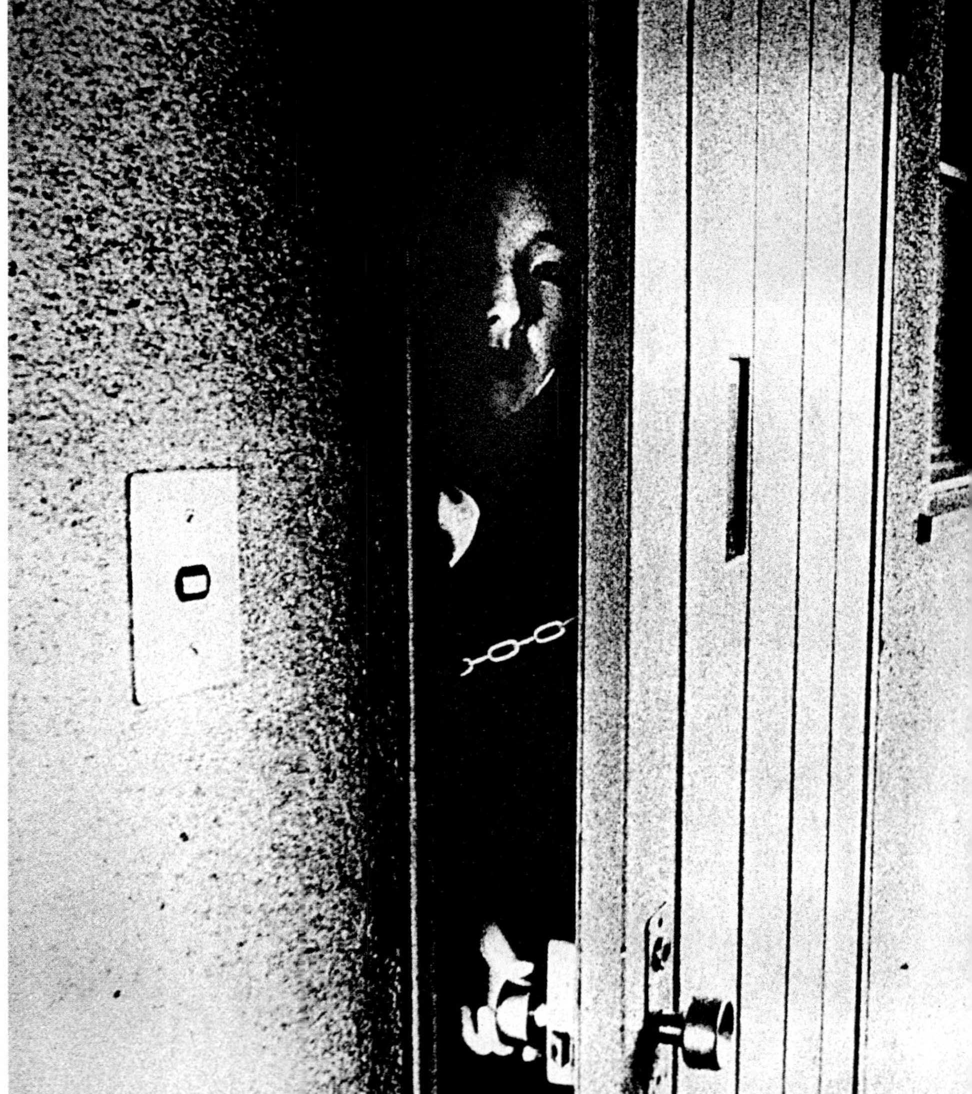

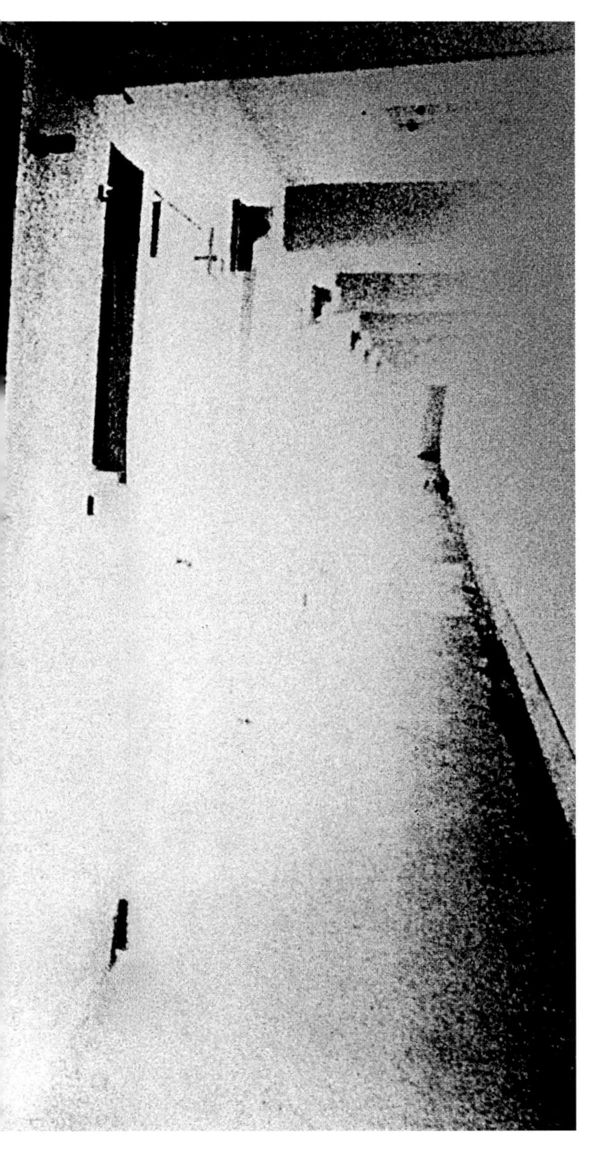

**(previous page) Apartment, Tokyo, Japan, 1967.** In the long corridor of a housing development, the door to one of the apartments is ajar. A chain is visible in the opening, below a suspicious face. The scene evokes a sense of emptiness and distance, fear and insecurity. At the same time, however, it is nonchalantly saturated in midday sun. The image can be read as a statement of intent. In classic documentary, the idea was to brush away all obstacles to seeing and to give as clear an account of the subject as possible. In this instance, however, the subject declines to emerge, preferring to keep to the shadows.

**Beach Boys, Zushi, Japan, 1967.** Youths smeared in sun tan lotion lie, like 'packed sardines' in Moriyama's words, on Shonan Beach in Zushi, where he was living at the time. He often shot a number of similar objects arranged in echelon like this. Moriyama was one of the first photographers to reflect on overcrowding and the loss of individuality in contemporary life. Oiled and inert, his subjects represent a degree-zero of self-indulgence. In the new postwar Japan, this kind of carnality was at variance with the stricter ethics of the old order. Japanese photographers were fascinated by the contrast.

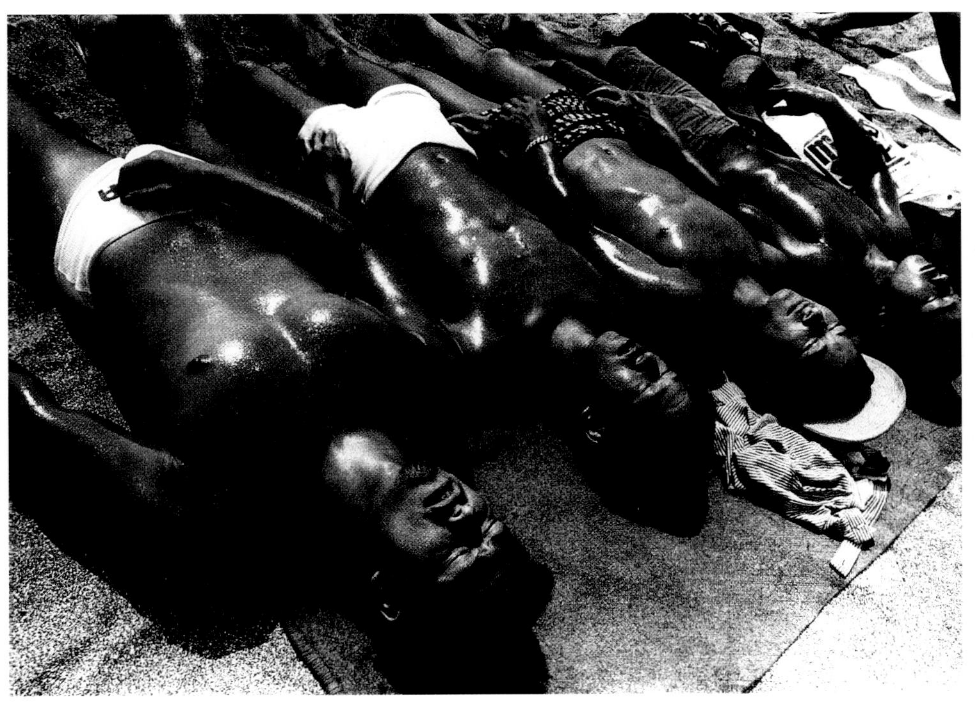

**Baton Twirls, Tokyo, Japan, 1967.** Moriyama may have encountered this scene as he stepped from a coffee shop somewhere around Jiyugaoka, where he had made a break on his journey from Zushi to Tokyo, on the suburban Toyoko Line. These uniformed high-steppers in their *shako* caps represent the new Japan, infiltrated by American influences of all sorts. Although others saw this as cultural contamination, Moriyama appears to have been non-judgemental.

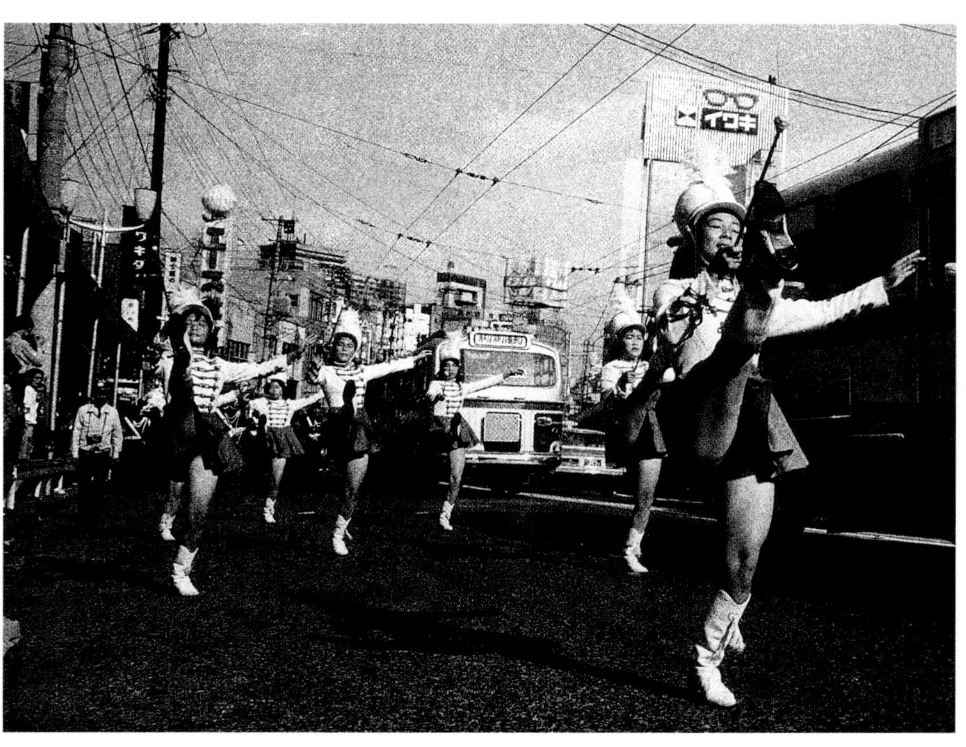

イワキ
ワキタ

**Tyres, Yokkaichi, Japan, 1968.** Around the time of this image, Moriyama, fascinated by Jack Kerouac's novel *On the Road*, began travelling himself, shooting all over the country. These are the tyres of a large lorry seen from a low angle and abstractly splattered, like a Jackson Pollock, with lime or paint. The picture resembles an infra-red image, as if responsive to a whirl of heat and energy. Moriyama's art as a photographer is characterized by the bold choice of such radical motifs as this – motifs to which we must bring our own readings.

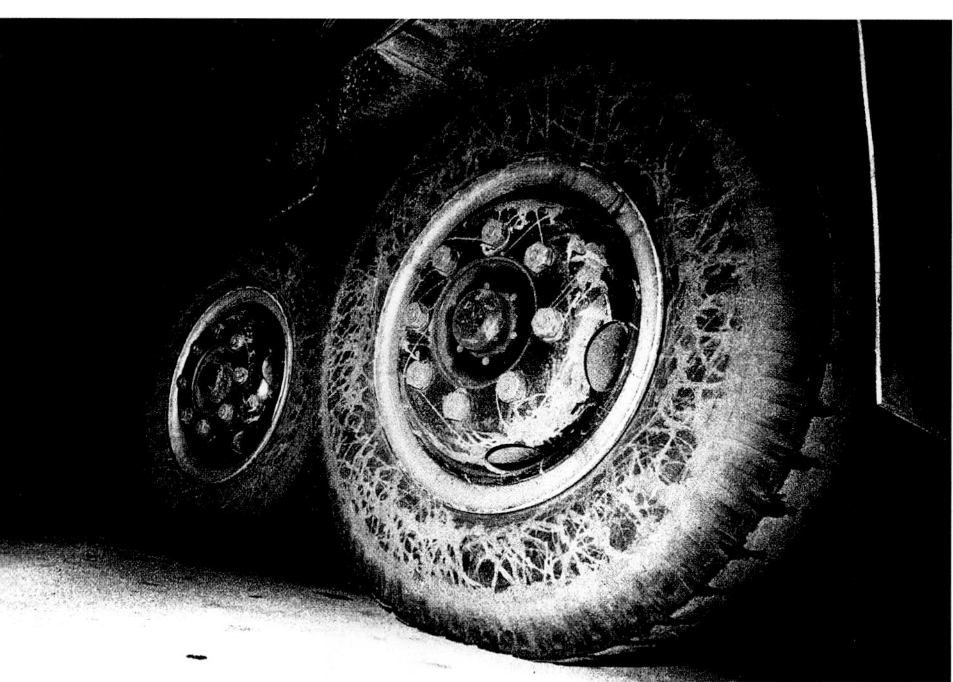

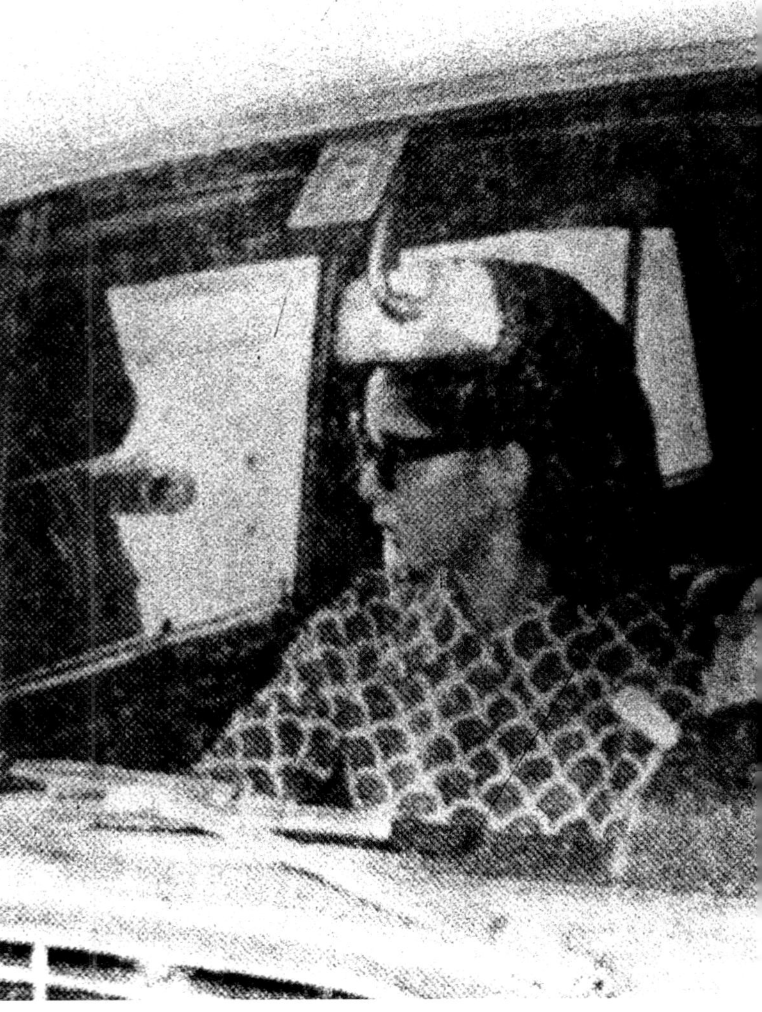

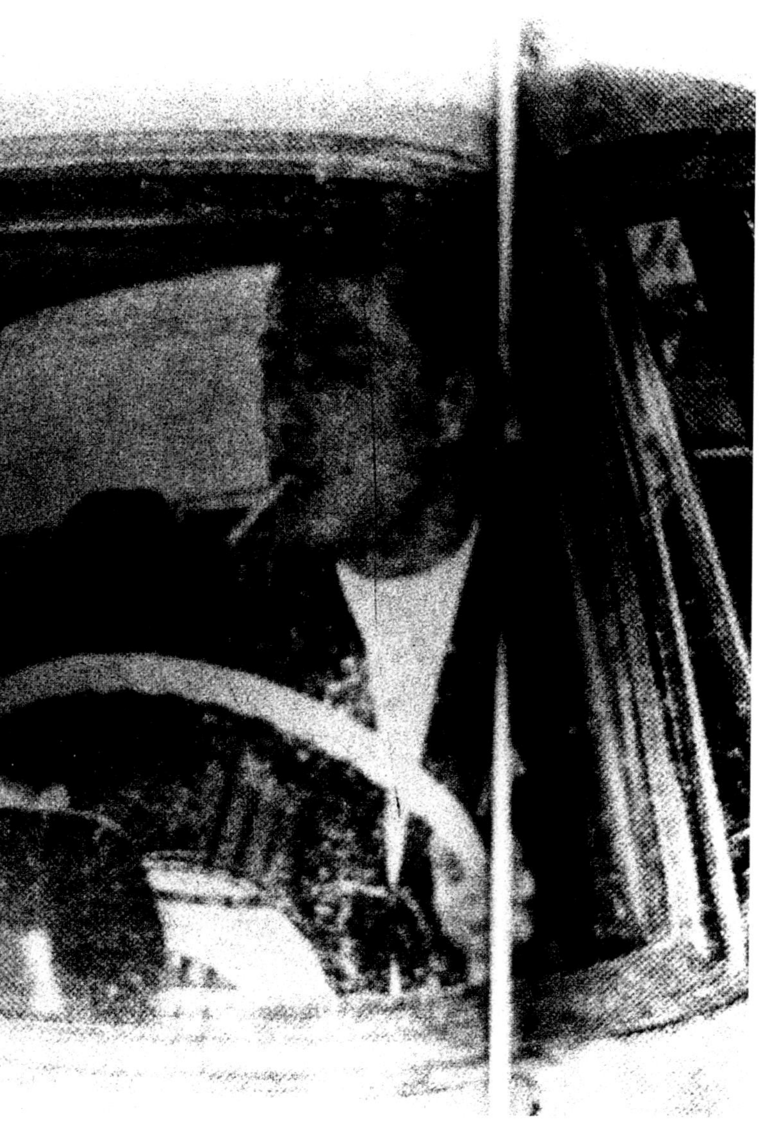

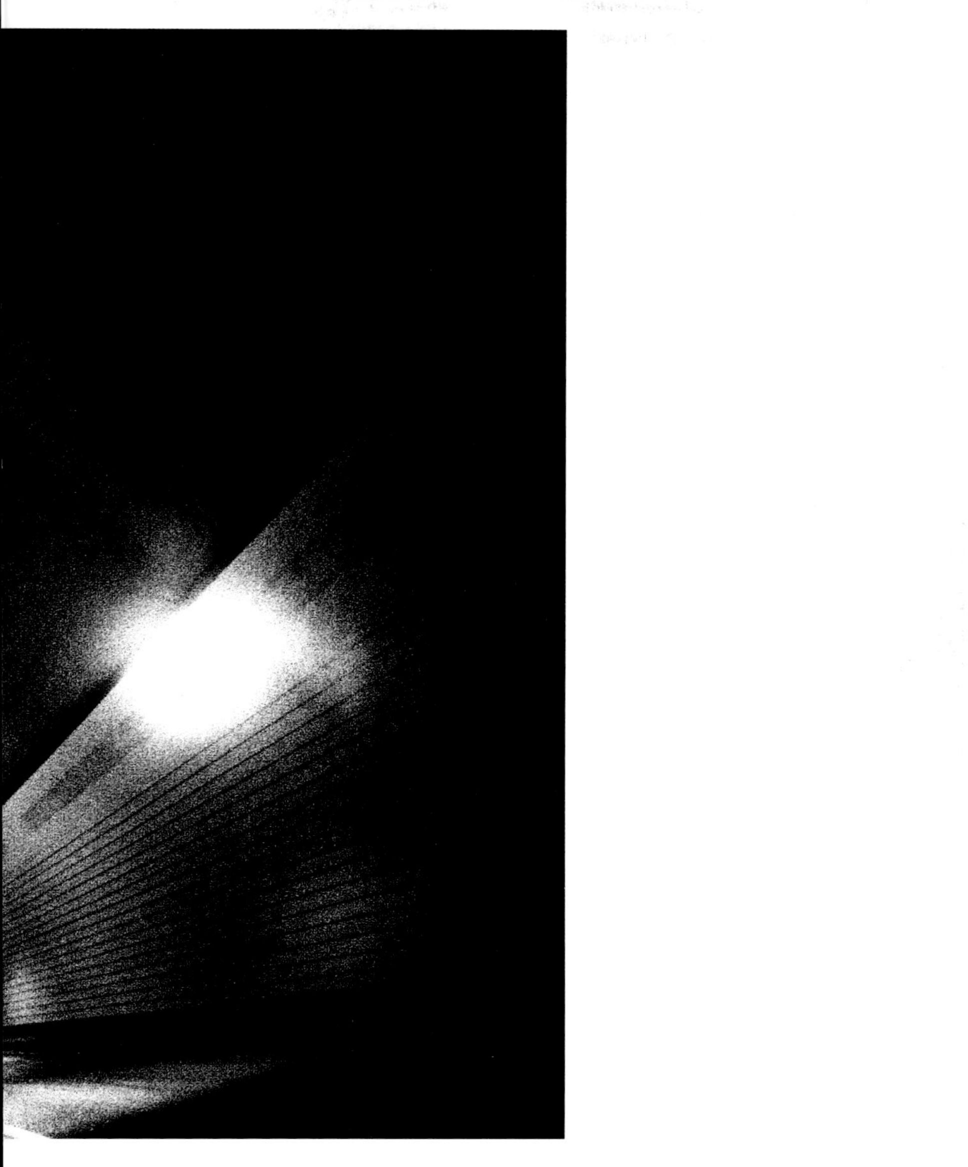

**(previous page) Highway, Shizuoka, Japan, 1969.** Up to this time, photographers had assumed that topographic pictures should be of particular, named places. It was unthinkable that one should set out to photograph nowhere in particular or the intervals between sites, even though so much of postmodern life is spent in such non-places. In this respect, this is a pioneering image, and one whose example was taken to heart by a new generation of photographers in the 1990s. Exclusion is the key to Moriyama's aesthetic: a journey with no destination, an event without outcome, or so far removed from the present moment as to be unknowable.

**Jetty, Chiba, Japan, 1969.** On 3 May 1969 a long-line tuna vessel capsized in heavy seas at the mouth of the River Tone in Choshi, Chiba. Eleven men perished. Moriyama went twice to the scene, once on the seventh day after the wreck, and again a week later, on the *shonanoka* – when special Buddhist rituals are performed. People had silently gathered on a jetty. Probably, they had no particular relationship to the victims, but Moriyama recalls that he did not feel able to approach them taking this image with a telephoto lens. He was one of the first photographers to admit to this kind of indirectness or belatedness as a characteristic of our lives. Events have, for the most part, already taken place and as latecomers we can only access them in our imaginations.

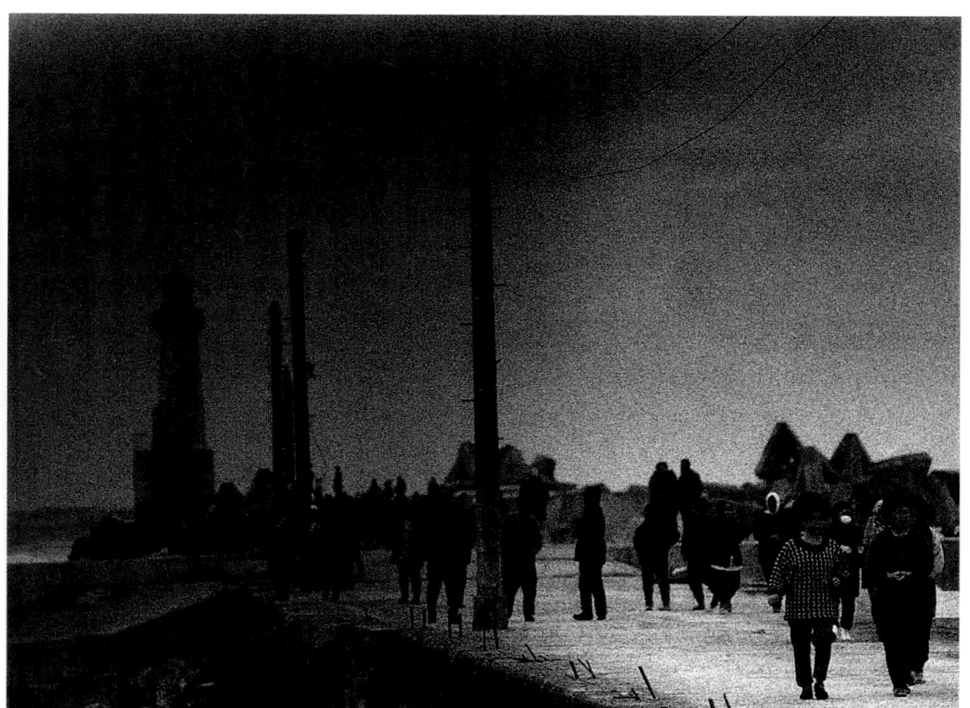

**On the Bed II, Tokyo, Japan, 1969.** The photographer Nobuyoshi Araki apparently questioned Moriyama as to why he left this woman unidentified, claiming that a photograph of a woman should always reveal her face. Moriyama is said to have replied that it was his 'samurai's mercy', meaning that he preferred not to brag about his romantic conquests. It is as if he had set out to describe the realities of love-making as a penumbral blur, or as a symbolic event, dimly articulated. He seems to have been intrigued by what cannot easily be expressed; by feelings, rather than the minute description of phenomena.

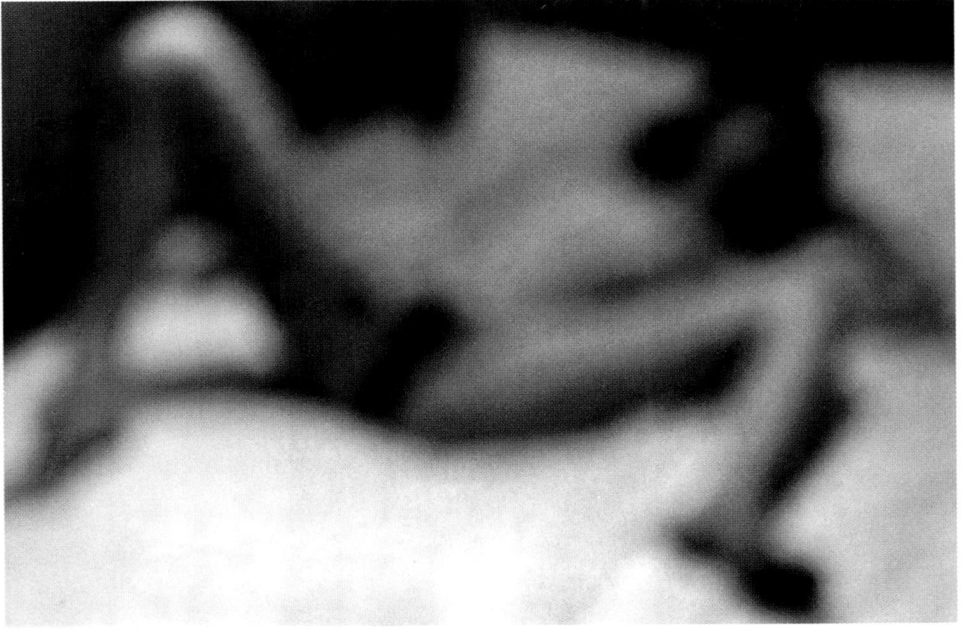

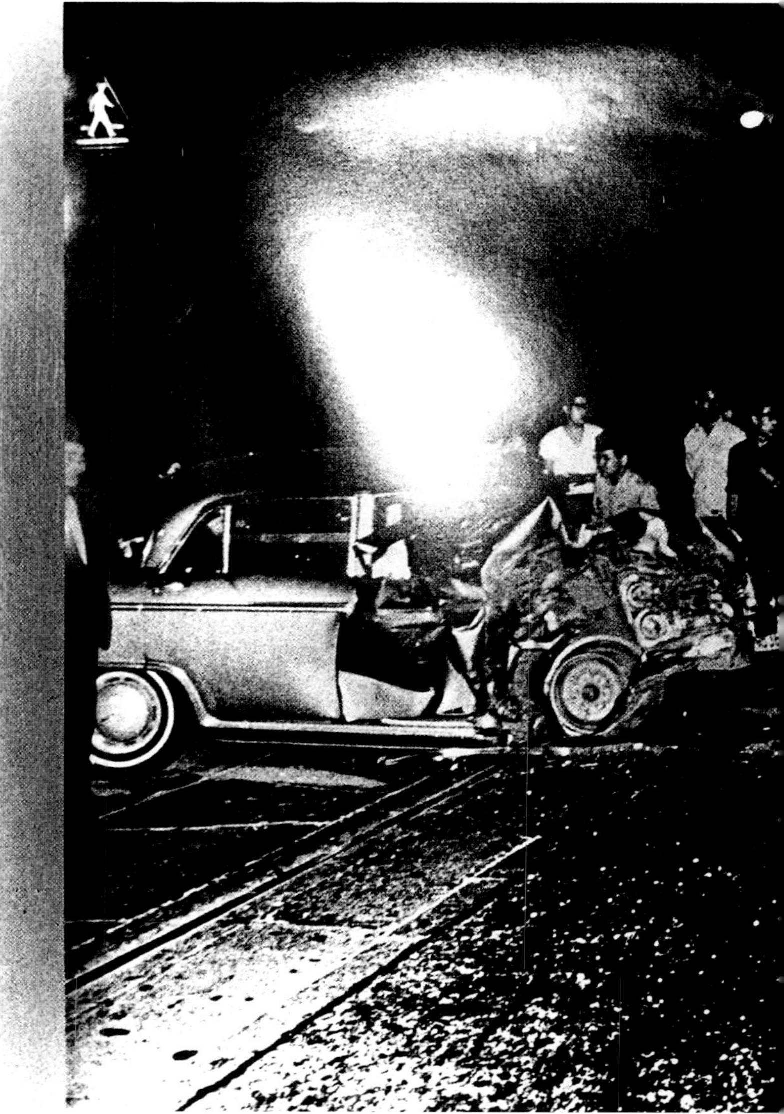

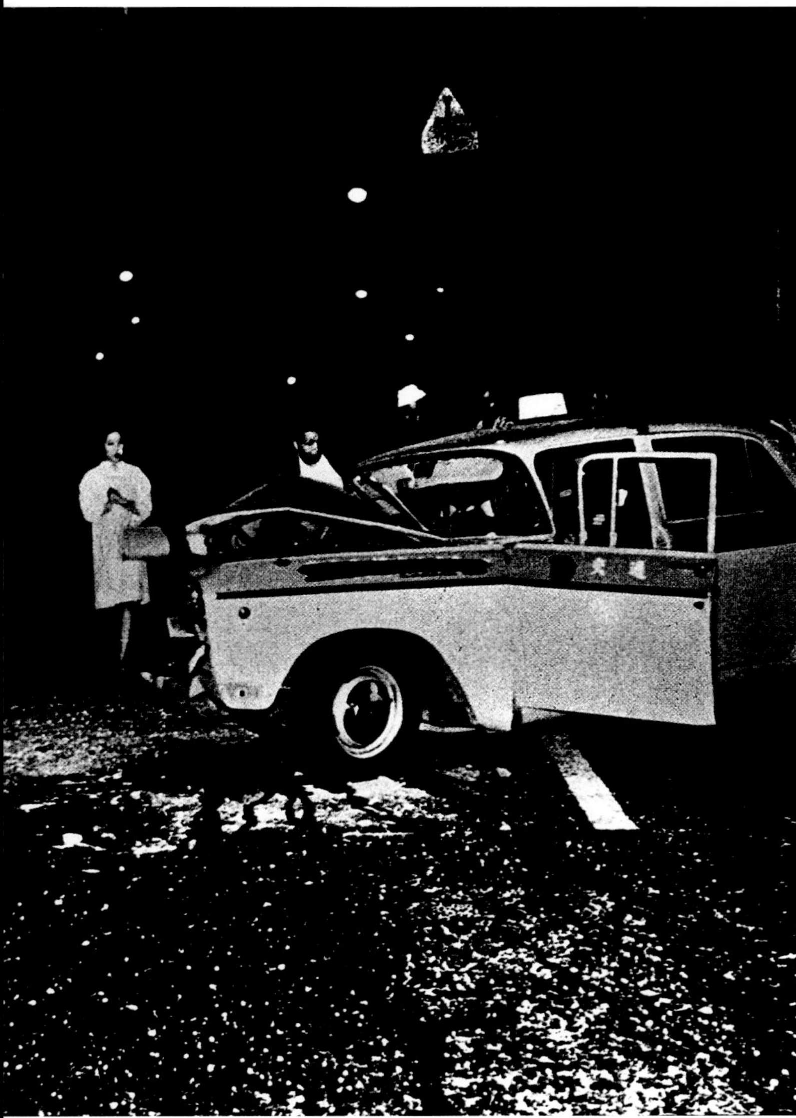

**(previous page) Car Crash, Tokyo, Japan, 1969.** This picture was rephotographed from a road-safety poster, intended to promote an awareness of dangerous driving. Moriyama was so impressed by the power of the original that he applied to the National Police Agency for a copy. He had witnessed many accidents while on the road, and he said he wished to use the poster's high contrast to evoke a sense of a reality that was both 'wondrous and shocking'. Warhol's famous car 'Accident' silkscreens of 1963 were repeated motifs of crashes and casualties. Moriyama, by contrast, has selected a moment at which survivors and passers-by survey the evidence and reflect on an event fast receding into history.

**Riot, Tokyo, Japan, 1969.** The original title of this picture was *10.21* – 21 October, then recognized as International Anti-War Day. Students in the anti-government movement Zenkyoto and young labourers in the Anti-War Youth Committee clashed with riot squads, demanding the return of Okinawa and the non-renewal of the US–Japan Security Treaty. This picture was taken underneath the railway viaduct on Yasukuni Street in Shinjuku. Typically, little can be made out clearly, which would reflect the experience of rioting on the night-time streets of a modern city. Student riots, with their generalized aims, seemed at the time to be expressions of the zeitgeist and could not be explained in conventional terms of cause and effect.

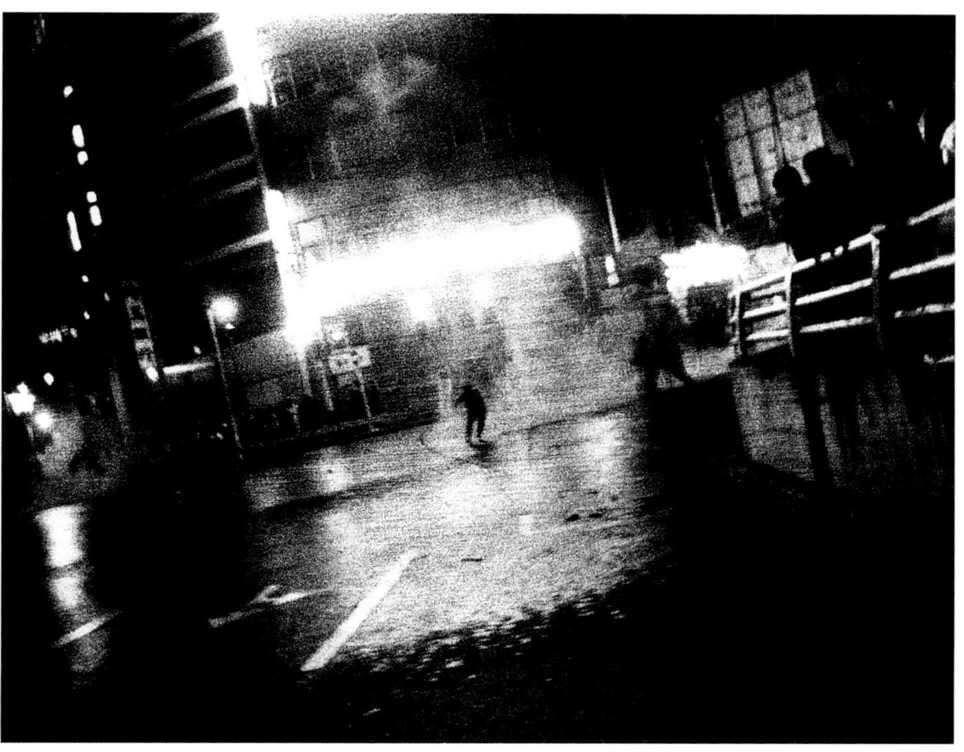

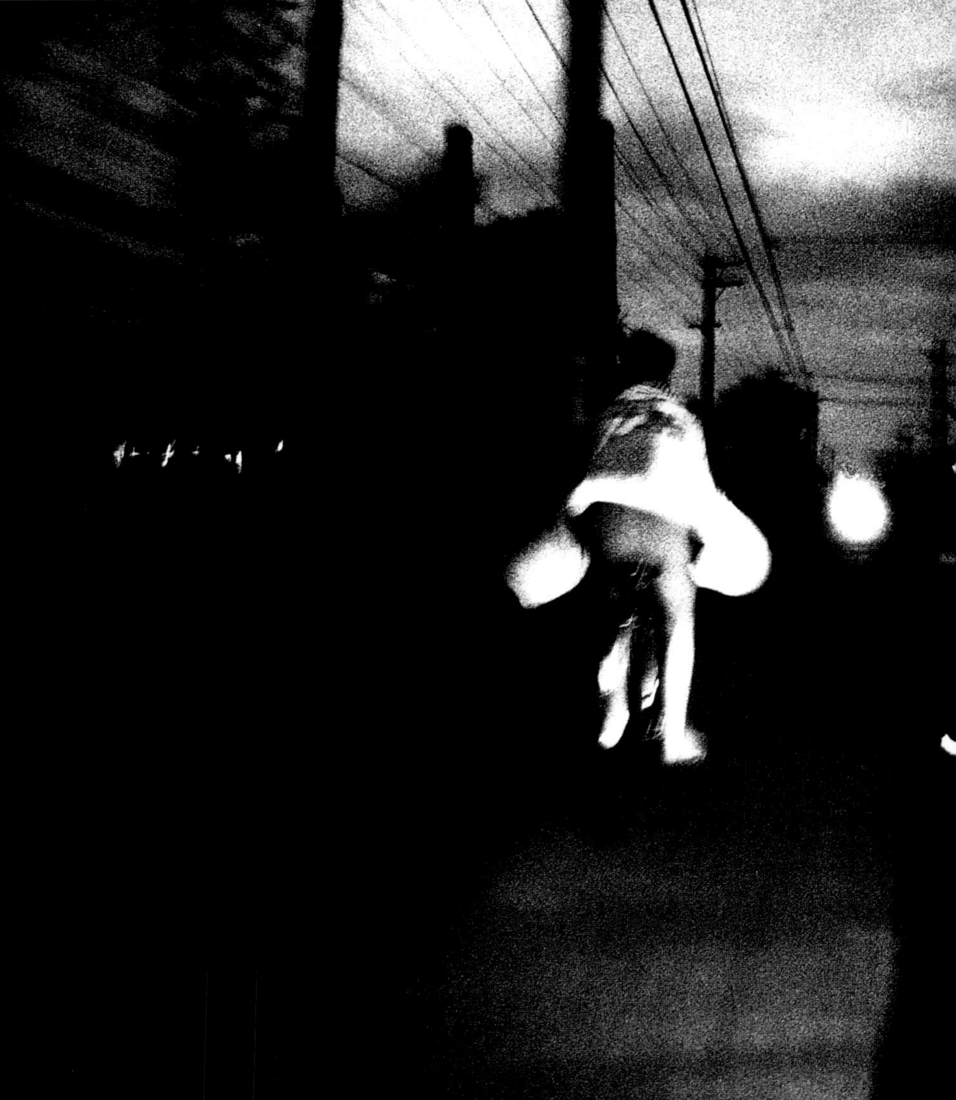

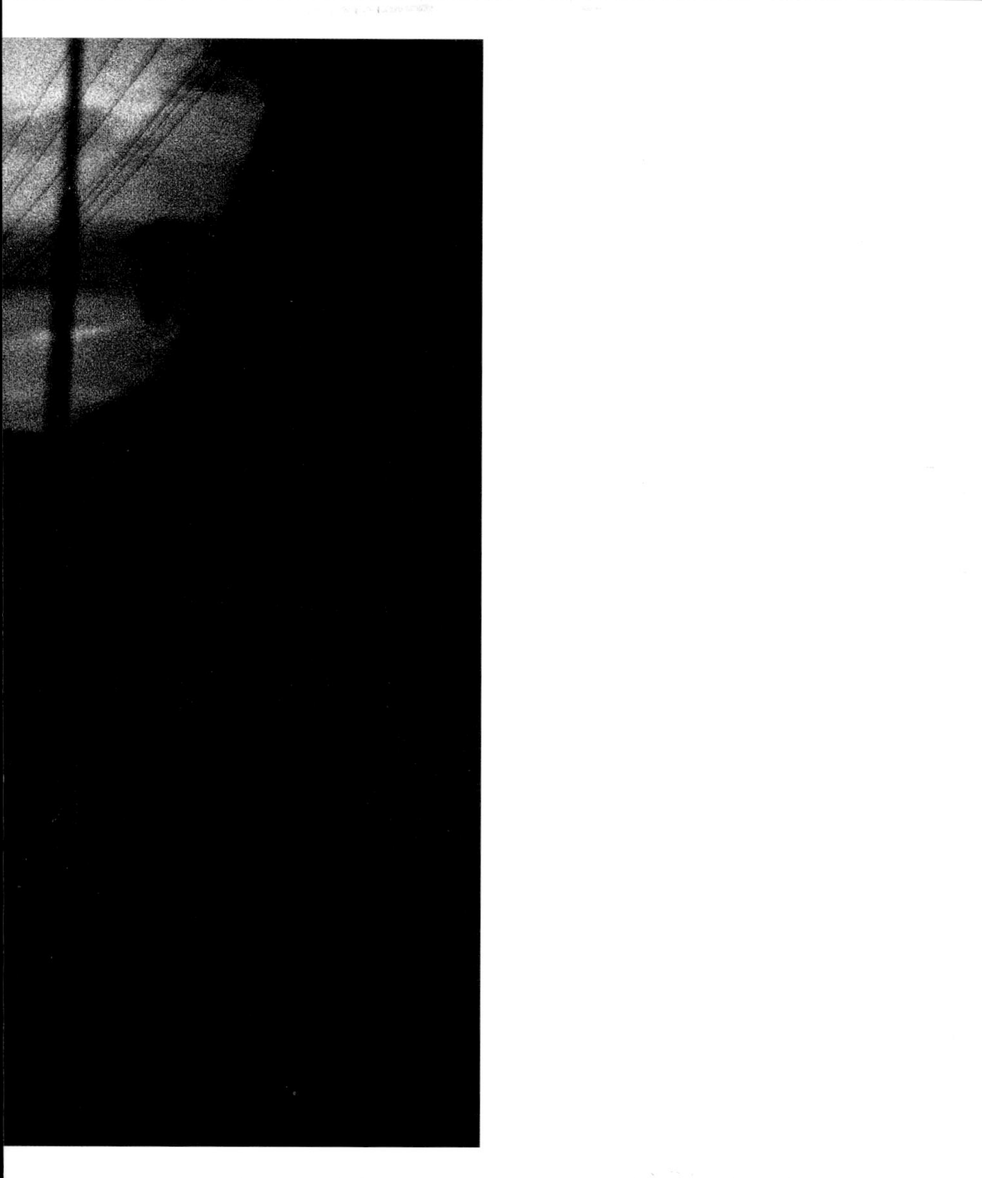

**(previous page) Afterglow, Kanagawa, Japan, 1969.** Taken from a passing car, this picture reflects on the subject's vulnerability to accident or malice. It also refers to the mentality of the driver – and by extension any individual – when suddenly confronted with circumstances that allow no room for reflection or considered judgement. It is not only events that are unfathomable in Moriyama's scheme of things, but consciousness itself.

**Yokosuka, Kanagawa, Japan, 1970.** A strobe light has been fired behind the woman, who flees down a narrow alley. There is a feeling of threatening pursuit and imminent danger hanging over the escaping woman. On a dangerous surface like this, she is unlikely to get far in her bare feet. What is she escaping from, dressed only in her slip at this time of night? Many of Moriyama's pictures resemble film stills, samples of narratives whose full story can only be guessed at.

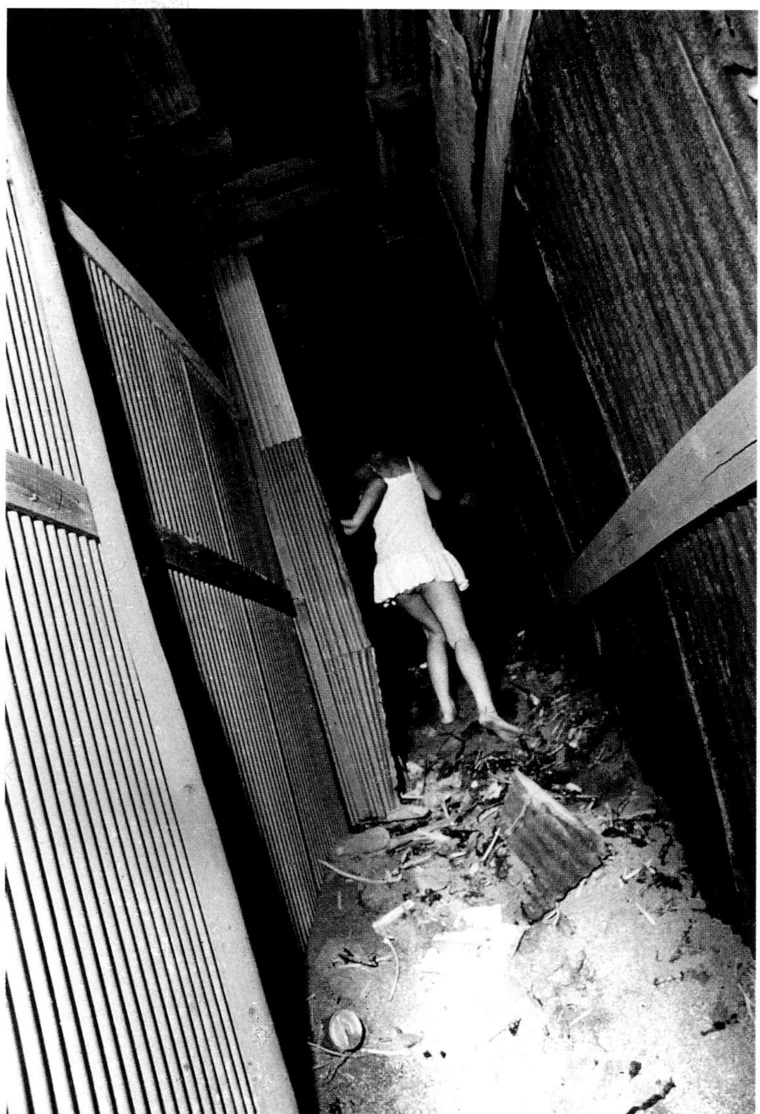

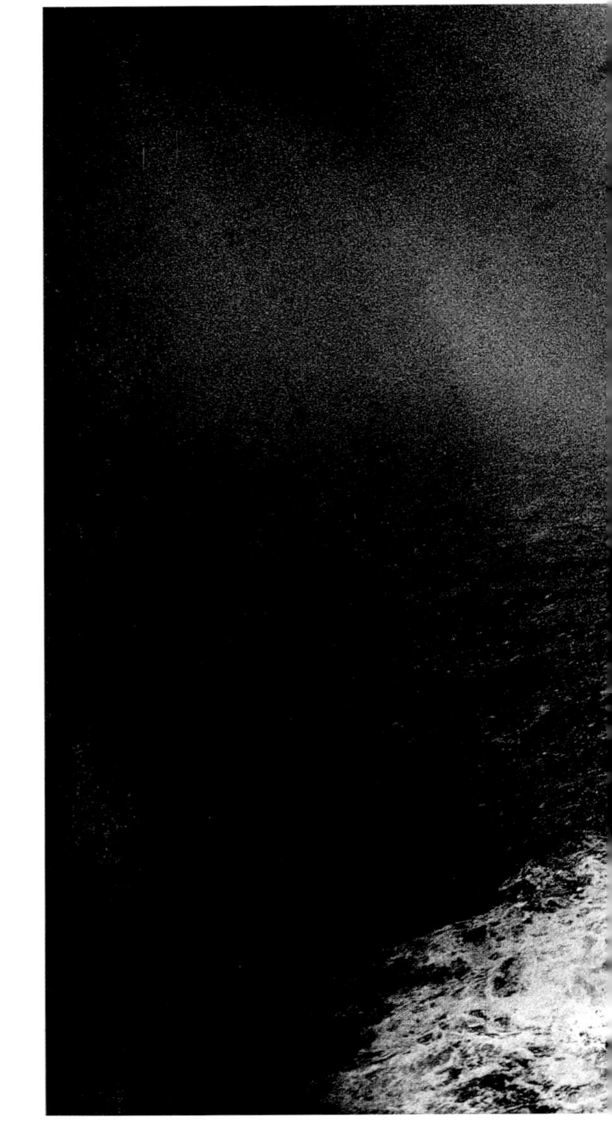

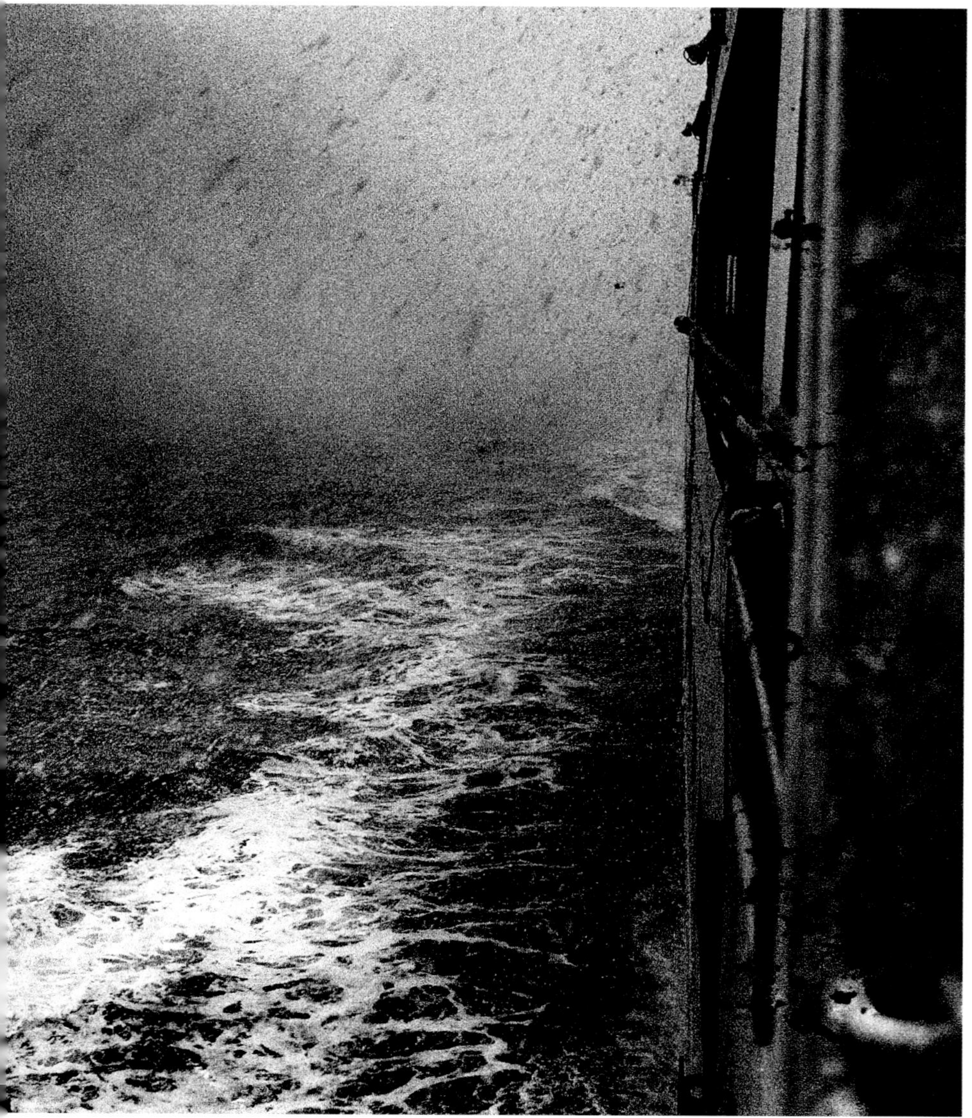

**(previous page) Straits, Hokkaido, Japan, 1970.** This view of the Straits of Tsugaru was taken aboard the ferry connecting Hakodate in Hokkaido with Aomori on the Japanese mainland. Hokkaido is home to Japan's disappearing indigenous people, the Ainu, and the Straits of Tsugaru have always been thought of as a border between cultures. One might therefore think of this picture as a contemplation on our passage through Time and History, leaving a wake that rapidly disappears into the darkness. It is also another instance of Moriyama's anonymous approach to place and identity, for such a picture might have been taken almost anywhere on the oceans of the world.

**Stray Dog, Aomori, Japan, 1971.** Two versions of this picture exist, printed with the dog facing in opposite directions. Moriyama went to Misawa in New Year 1971 and observed that it had much in common with many base towns, with its 'barbers, cabarets, boutiques, beauticians and oculists ... all lined up' and 'dogs everywhere'. Urban dogs were often featured in postwar European photography, fighting and snarling, symbolizing animality. Moriyama's dog, on the other hand, seems to have been taken from a kindred dog's-eye point of view, as if merely encountered rather than elevated into a symbolic order.

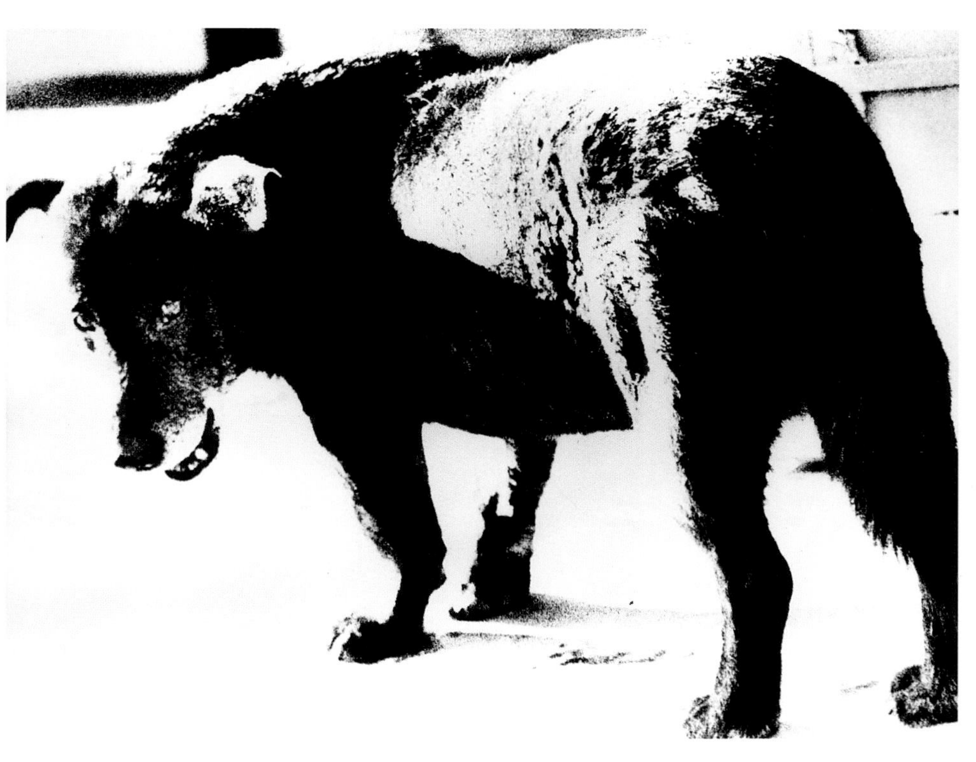

**On the Way Home, Ishikawa, Japan, 1971.** Boys, probably middle-school pupils, crouch at the roadside. Their sense of guilt at idling time away on their way home is almost tangible. Or perhaps the paper they are engrossed in contains a secret, which they would prefer to keep from the prying eyes of passing travellers. Once again, Moriyama chooses to reflect on the enigma of the unknowable or 'other'.

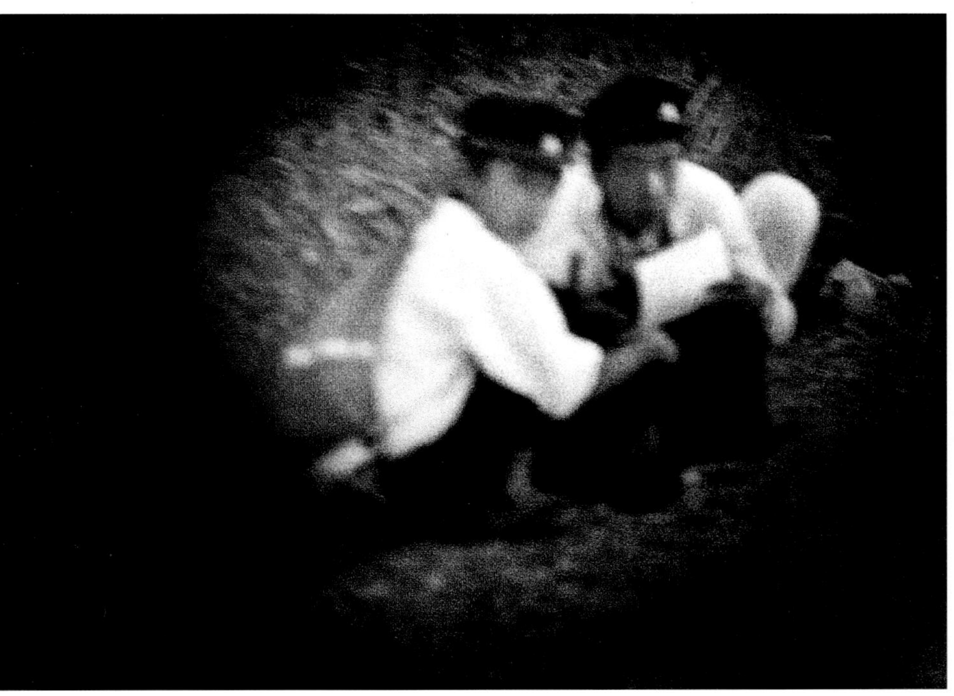

**City Street, Aomori, Japan, 1971.** Humanist artists from all cultures have remarked on the process of socialization – what happens to us as we mature and grow into our preordained social roles. Initially, we are amazed and distracted by the wealth of phenomena around us, but with time, we settle down and accept constraint. The child to the left in this group portrait or conversation piece appears to have opted for inwardness, perhaps in response to the cacophonous background.

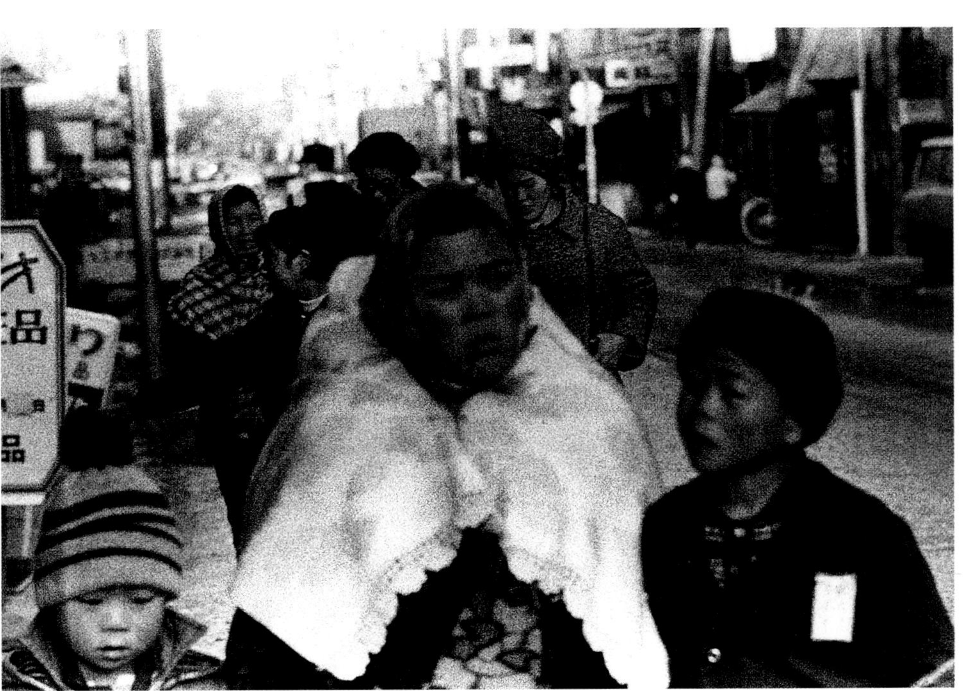

**After School, Ishikawa, Japan, 1971.** Another child, also in a world of her own, is captured in this photograph. Taken in passing, she is one of the most oblivious of all Moriyama's subjects. Conceivably, the stony road ahead represents a life unwinding, but it might just as easily stand for a future in which she will be soon forgotten. This highly detached style, focusing on insignificance, infiltrated the photographic mainstream in the 1980s. Moriyama was one of its first exponents, and one of the most radical.

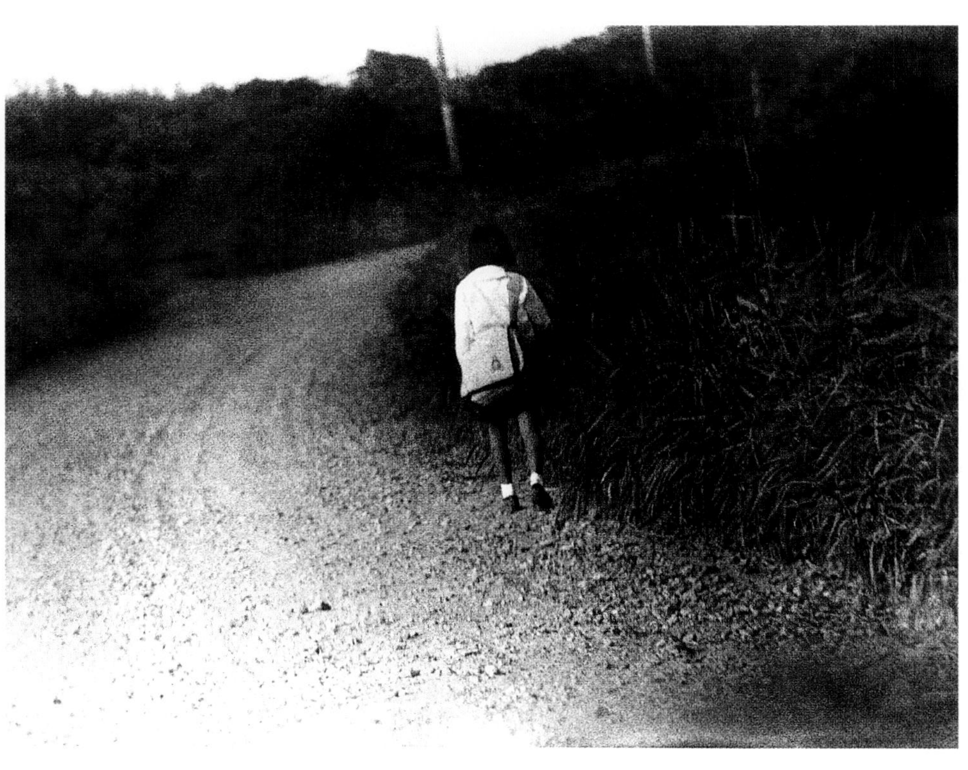

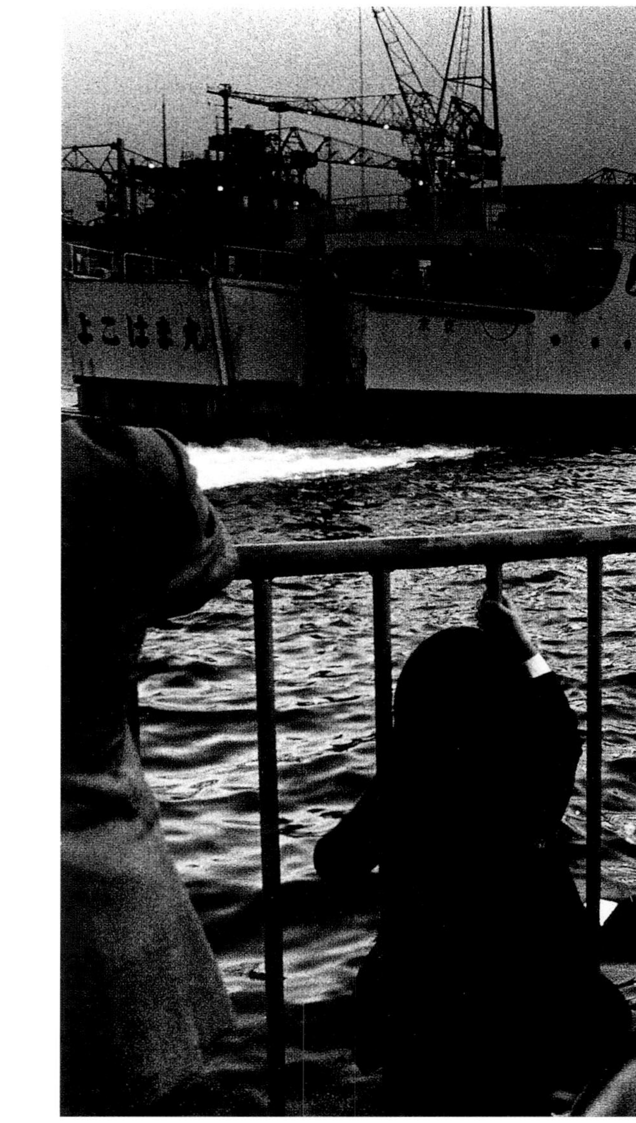
よこはま丸

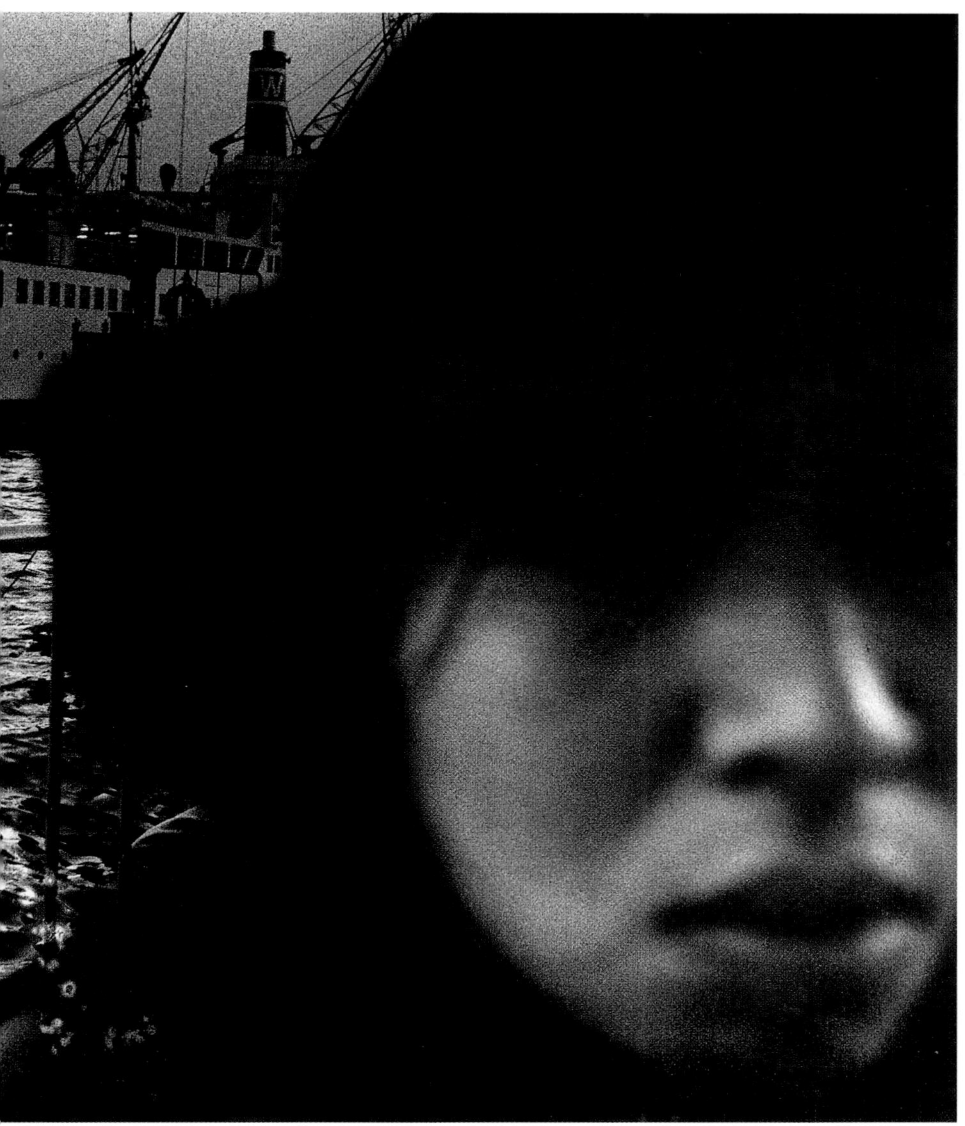

**(previous page) Quay, Kanagawa, Japan, 1971.** Moriyama's image was inspired by the line from Shin'ichi Mori's song 'Harbour Town Blues': 'As I peer across the straits, standing on tiptoe ...' However, while the song refers to the Straits of Tsugaru, careful inspection of this photograph reveals the name of the ship in the background as *Yokohama Maruth*, suggesting that the picture was taken off the coast at Yokohama and that the ferry is only making the crossing of Tokyo Bay to nearby Chiba. Moriyama's is at heart a romantic art, full of a yearning for revelation, hence his constant interest in the lure of illumination. For a visionary of his order, one white ship will serve as well as another.

**New York, USA, 1971.** Visible on the left is the head of one of the horses that pull the tourist carriages near Central Park in New York. Moriyama visited the city with the graphic designer Tadamori Yokoo. The camera used was a compact, half-sized 110mm, and the shot was probably taken from a taxi window. Moriyama was frightened of air travel and, according to Yokoo, never ventured out on his own in New York, spending most of his time in his room. This photograph evokes the sense of a hunted man in an alien environment, recalling the aesthetic of heist movies of the late 1960s. What is new about this sort of informal photography is that it expresses so little about the ostensible topic and so much about the artist's state of mind.

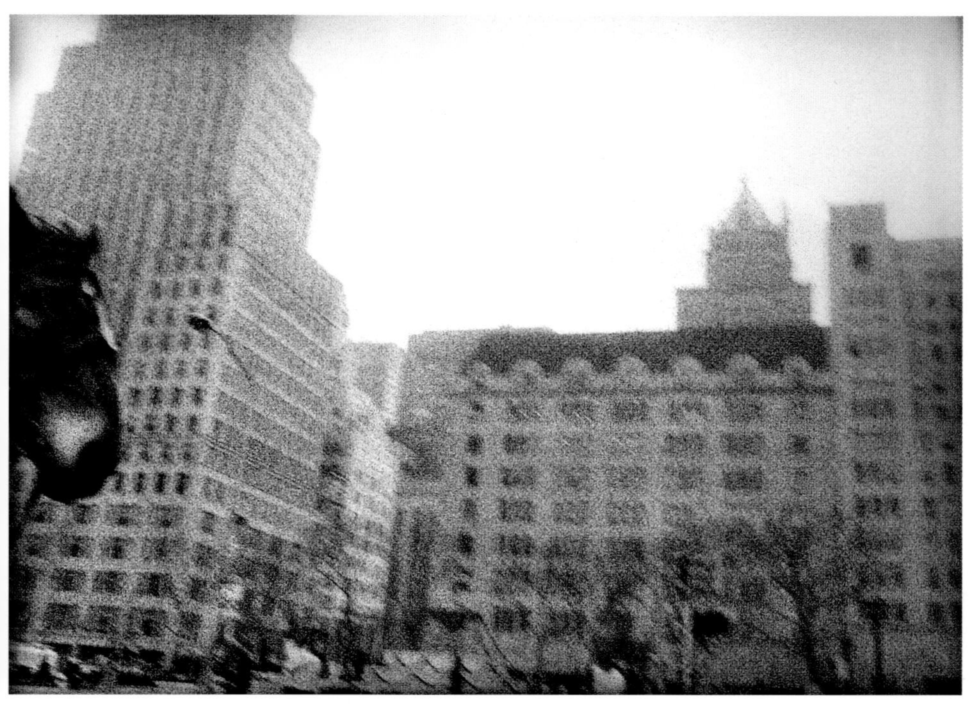

**Machine, Kanagawa, Japan, 1972.** This image comes from Moriyama's own magazine, *Records*. In an interview, he once listed what he called his 'Three Sacred Treasures' (punning on a concept of the Japanese Empire) as the motorcycle, jukebox and Christmas tree. Anyone familiar with the new American photography of the 1950s and 1960s – by Diane Arbus, Robert Frank, Danny Lyon and Gary Winogrand, for instance – will recognize these as important elements in the iconography of the period: signifying mobility, entertainment and kitsch ritual. Reflection and transparency, such as those one comes across in the shop windows of the big city – hinting at a virtual world of dreams and visions – fascinated photographers of that era.

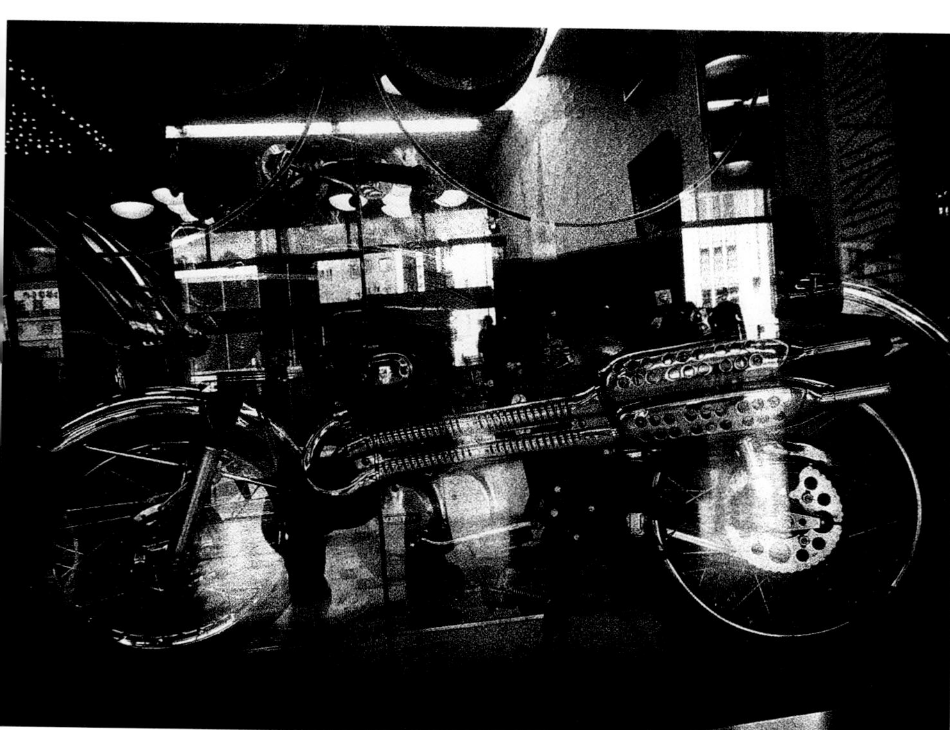

**Coal Mining Town, Hokkaido, Japan, 1973.** The place is Yubari, where there was an old coal mine, opened in the Meiji era (1868–1912). It was one of the major mining districts and supported Japan's modernization, until coal gave way to oil in the 1960s. A documentarist might have given a detailed and legible account of the decay of Yubari; Moriyama chose to find a figure and a mood expressive of abandonment and assimilation into darkness.

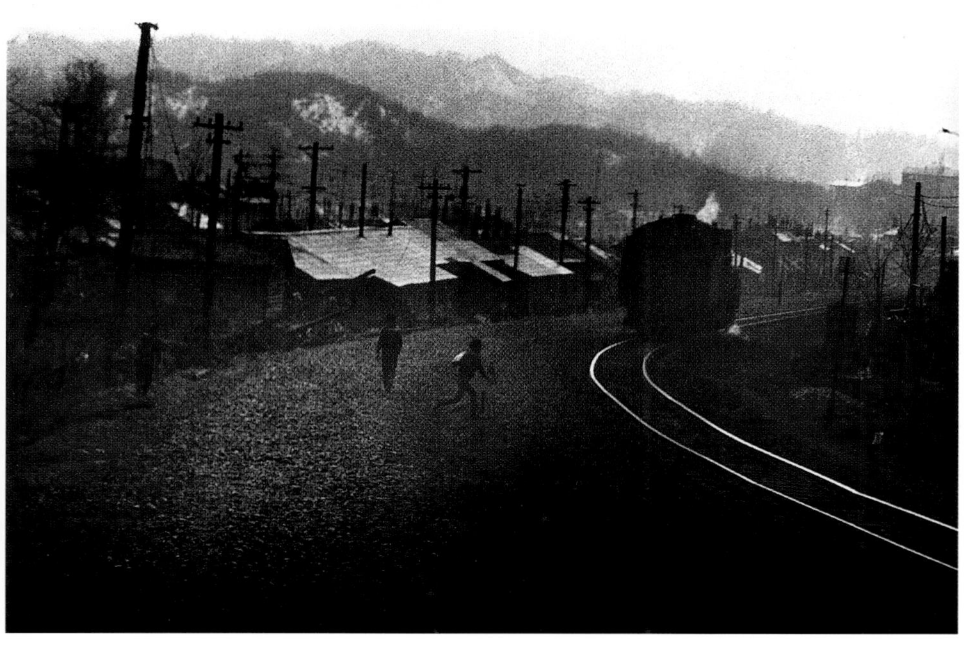

**Cabbage, Nagano, Japan, 1974.** This picture was shot in a cabbage patch in Saku, Nagano, where Moriyama used to go each summer to teach on a residential photography course. Close-ups of plant life recur in modernist photography as it evolved in the 1920s and 1930s. Cabbages, intricately veined, stood for the complexity of Nature. For the most part, such intricate miracles were photographed in a revealing, clinical light. Moriyama's interest, however, has always been in the dynamics of perception, in whirls and swirls too rapid to be taken in, or a sudden and slippery recession into the vortex.

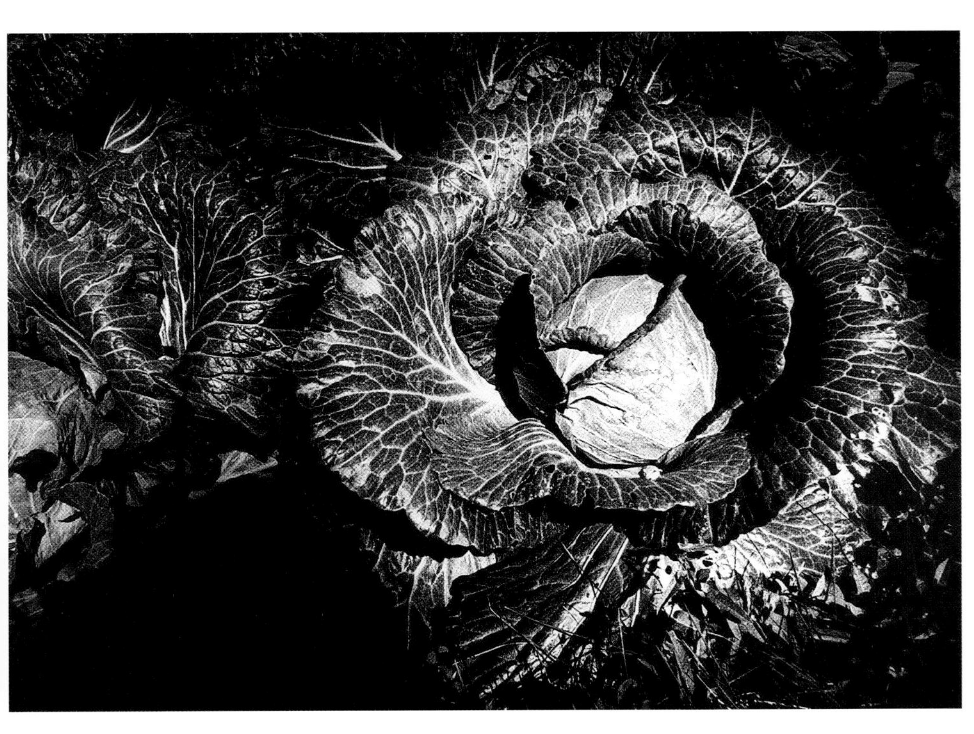

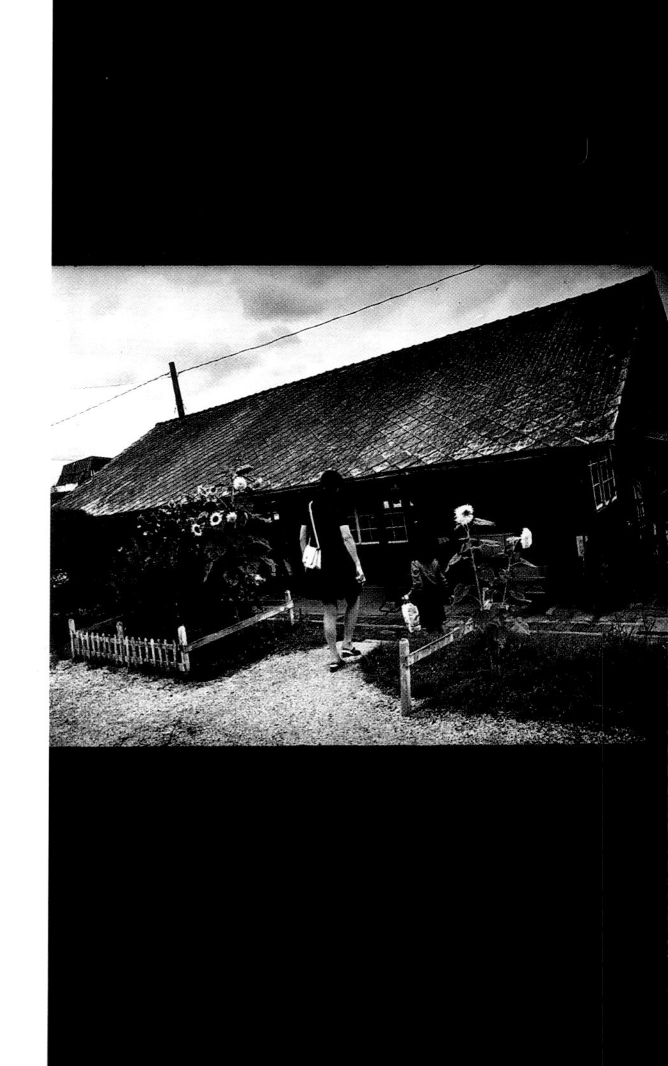

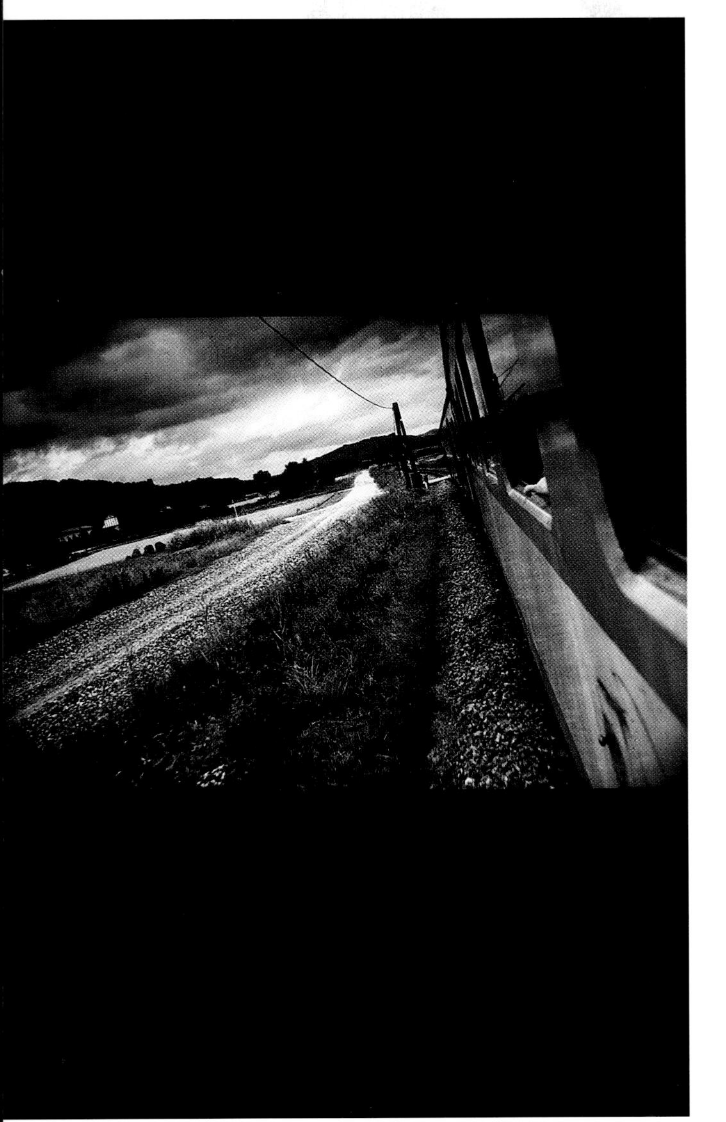

**(previous page) Tono, Iwate, Japan, 1974.** Moriyama went to the town of Tono, inspired by the book *Tales of Tono*, compiled by the great ethnologist Kunio Yanagita in the 1930s. The name 'Tono', which means 'faraway fields', 'brought about romantic images, even before I had ever seen it', he recalled. In Tono, old tales had been handed on from generation to generation by storytellers, and most involved apparitions and phantoms. Moriyama's own *Tales of Tono* came out in 1974 as a small pocket book of paired 35mm pictures, as here. The picture-taking was carried out in three days and presents Tono 'as found', with no attempt to edit out its non-folkloric aspects.

**Okinawa, Japan, 1975.** Okinawa was culturally and politically significant as an area of traditional Japan that was more or less under American occupation. Moriyama's interest here, however, is far removed from cultural and political issues, being concentrated simply on the art of making pictures. Drawn into the image, we might speculate that the two boys peering into the sun towards the photographer are brothers, and that the girl sharing bread with the boy to the left might be their older sister.

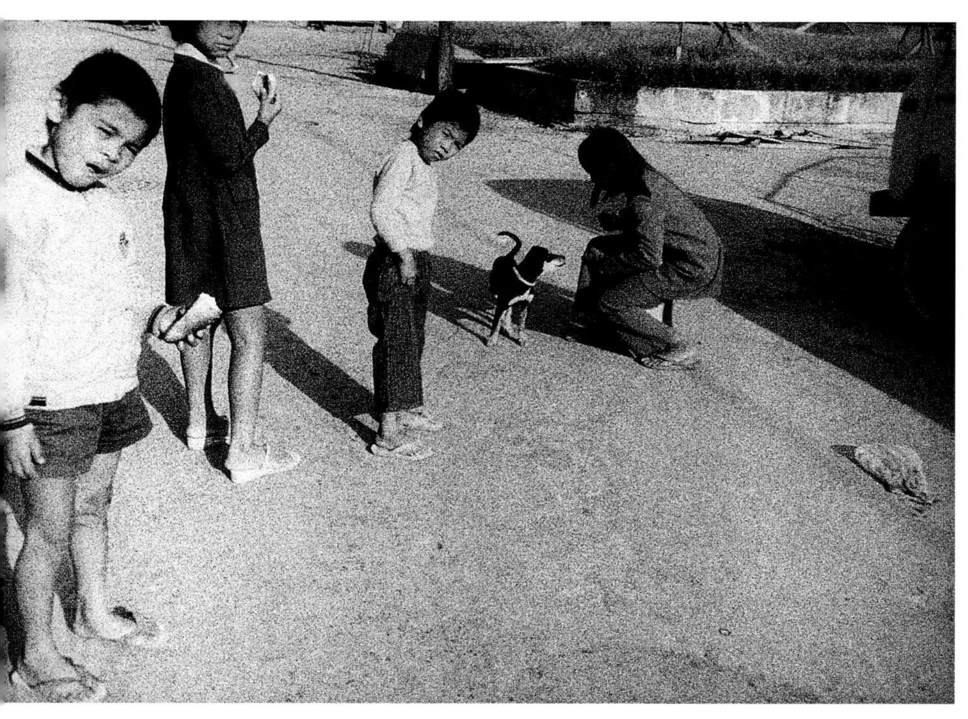

**Swine, Aomori, Japan, 1976.** This animal is a cross between a wild boar and a domestic pig. With more visible context it would be documentary picture, but cropped like this, the image becomes emblematic. Moriyama has always been impatient of clichés, however, and in this case the pig, with its keen senses and unprejudiced consumption of everything it finds around it, is perhaps intended to epitomize the strict empiricism that characterizes Moriyama's approach to phenomena.

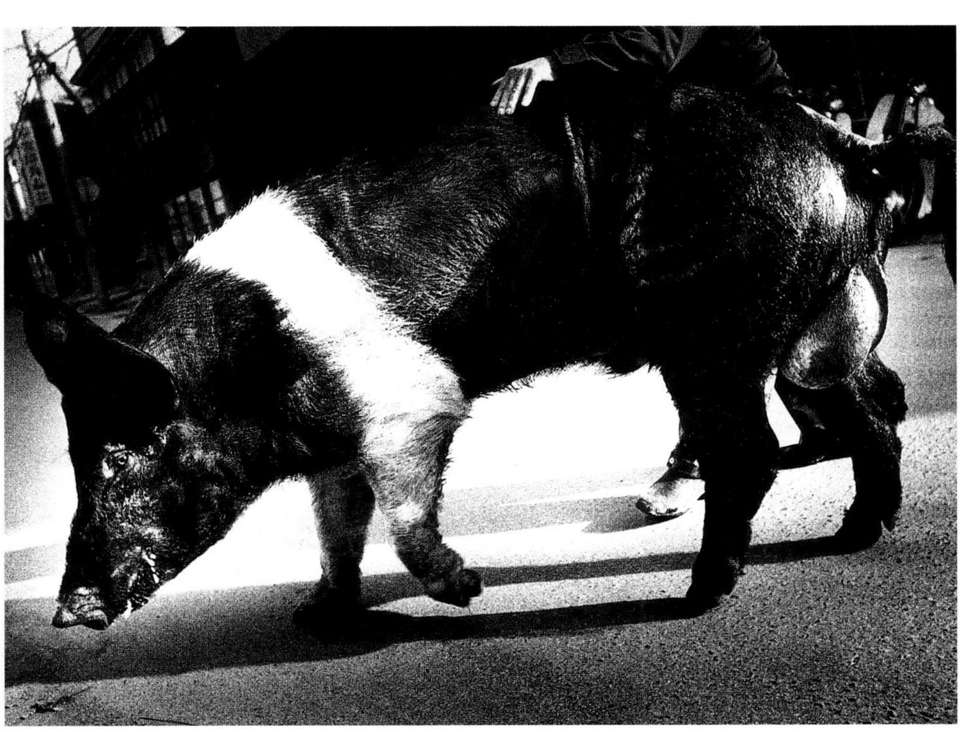

**Evening Scene, Aomori, Japan, 1977.** Aomori's Pepsi drinkers seem to have gone home, and the business of the day to have reached its conclusion. The shadows cast on the walls of buildings suggest that the sun is going down, leaving only evidence of the mundane activities of work and leisure. This is, of course, a documentary picture, but of a new kind, which presents the inhabited environment as a transitional zone crossed by wires, rails and tracks. This kind of disinterested approach to topography originated in the 1970s and was perfectly suited to Moriyama's outlook.

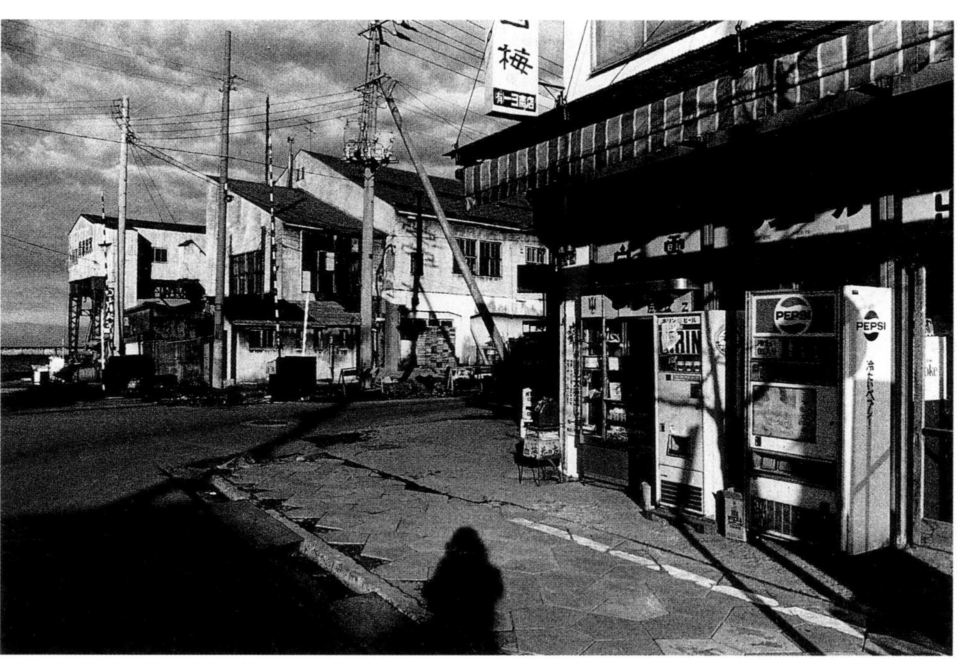
梅
PEPSI

**Hot Spring Resort, Gunma, Japan, 1979.** With their faces hidden, the anonymous men, all dressed in the same *yukata* (a relaxed evening kimono), evoke a slightly different version of the much-photographed Japanese 'salary man' culture. Objectively lit, this would have been a conventional group portrait. As it is, we are forced to gauge character from what we would normally think of as secondary evidence – posture and gesture, for example. Although nothing definite can be learnt from such evidence, we make the attempt anyway. Moriyama has always been interested in the encryption of photographs, in their suggestive rather than their descriptive capabilities.

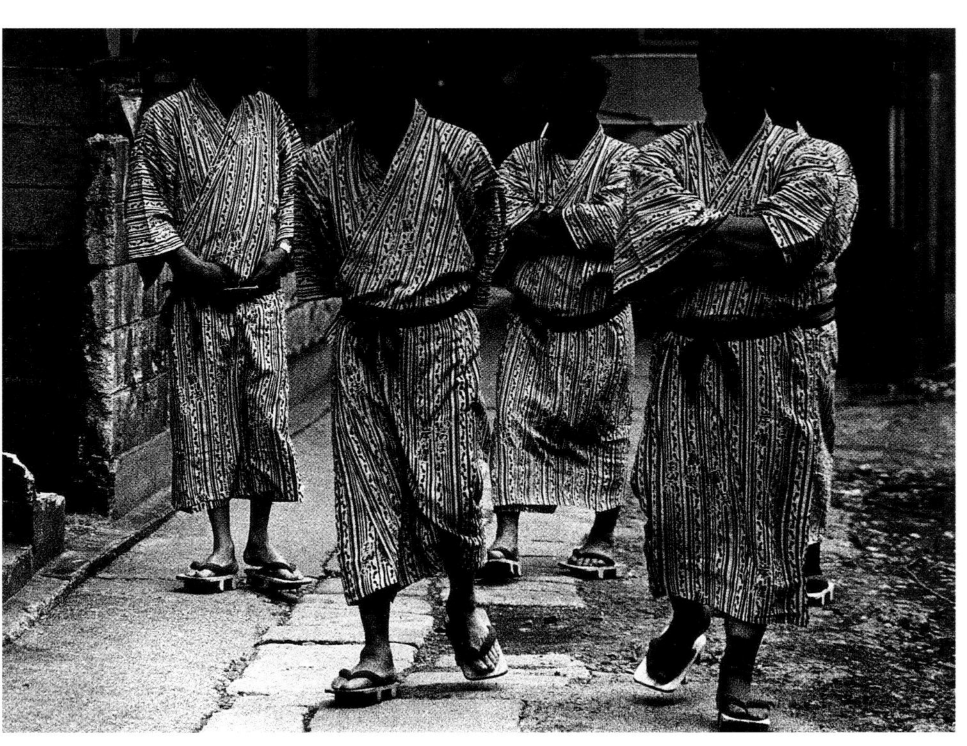

**Fedora, Tokyo, Japan, 1980.** This photograph of a hat, a favourite subject for Moriyama, was published in *Light and Shadow* in 1982. The hat's felt folds and dark, defining band are sculpturally impressive. It appears to be relatively new, or at least unsoiled. Even so, it has been pressed and shaped to its owner's specifications, and we can easily imagine how the prow of the crown would feel to the hand. Like the picture of the kimono-clad 'salary men' (page 85), this hat, by inference, points intriguingly to the personality of its owner.

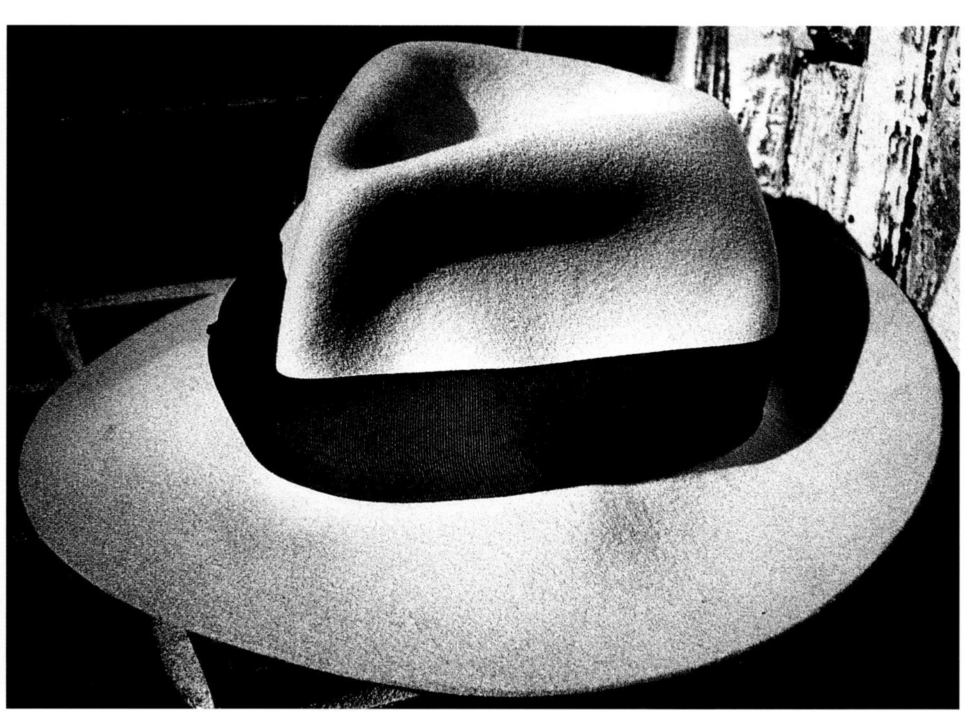

**Cypresses, Kanagawa, Japan, 1980.** Photographed at this oblique angle, these cypress trees appear to have been shaped by the wind, just as a sandy shore is sculpted by the receding tide. A scene with trees under an open sky would constitute a landscape but in the absence of any familiar context, we are obliged to look twice before recognizing these splintering, textured surfaces, which could equally be frost or fire. Black-and-white photography, in particular, has this power to transform and cast into doubt – a quality to which Moriyama has always been attracted.

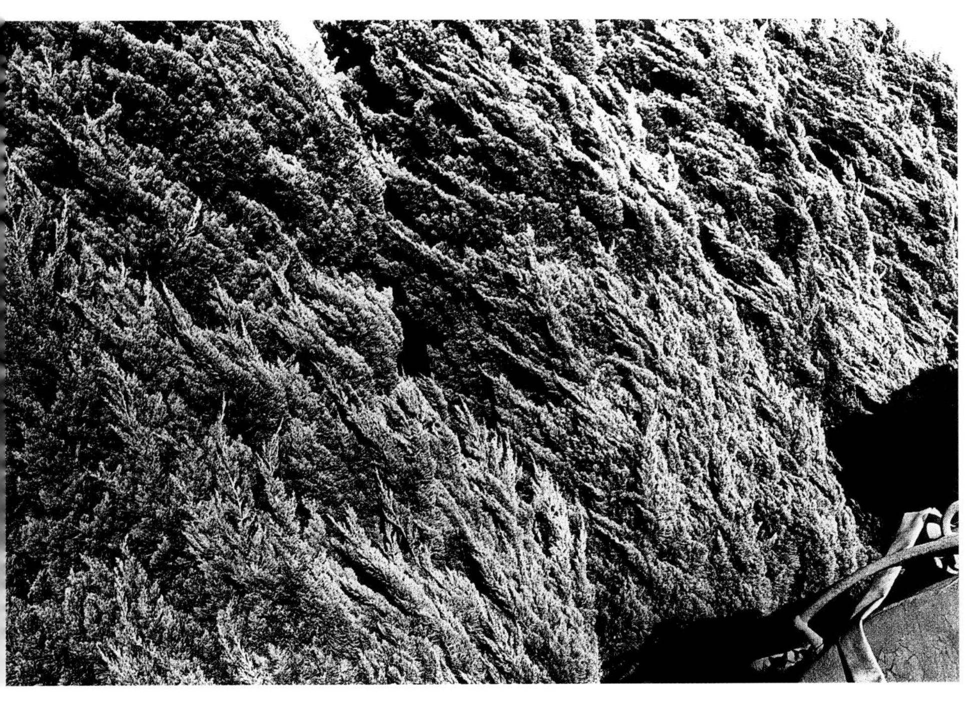

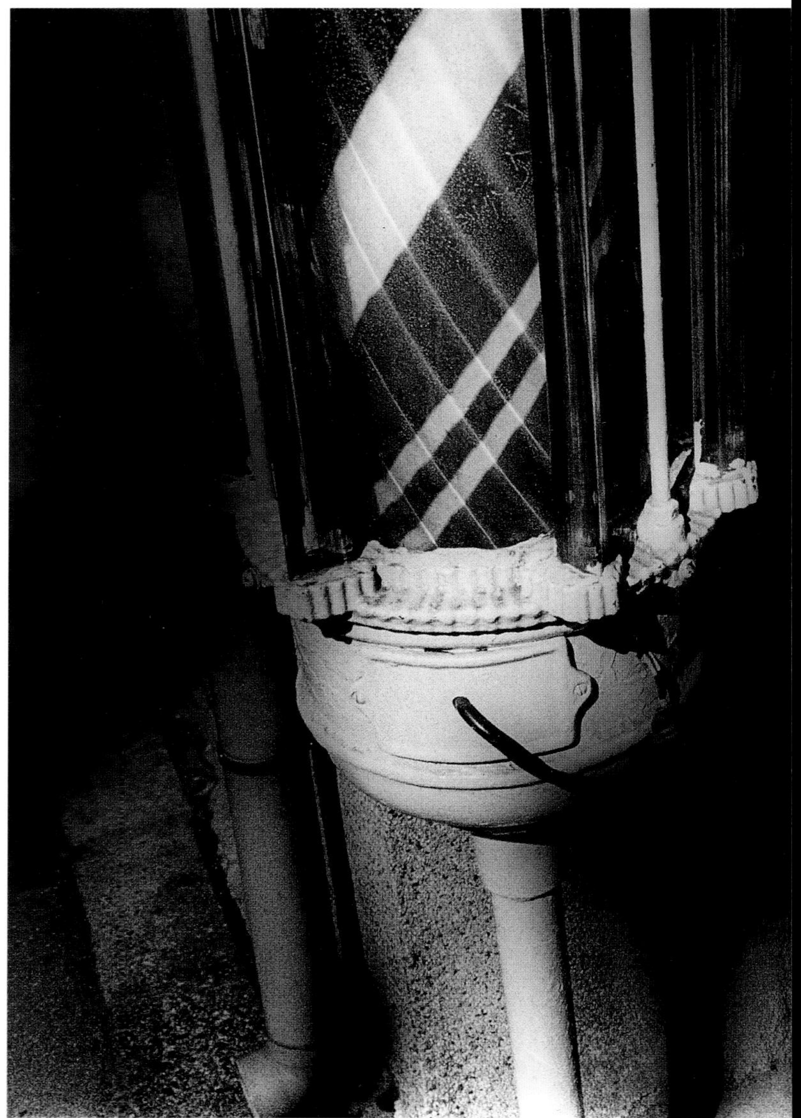

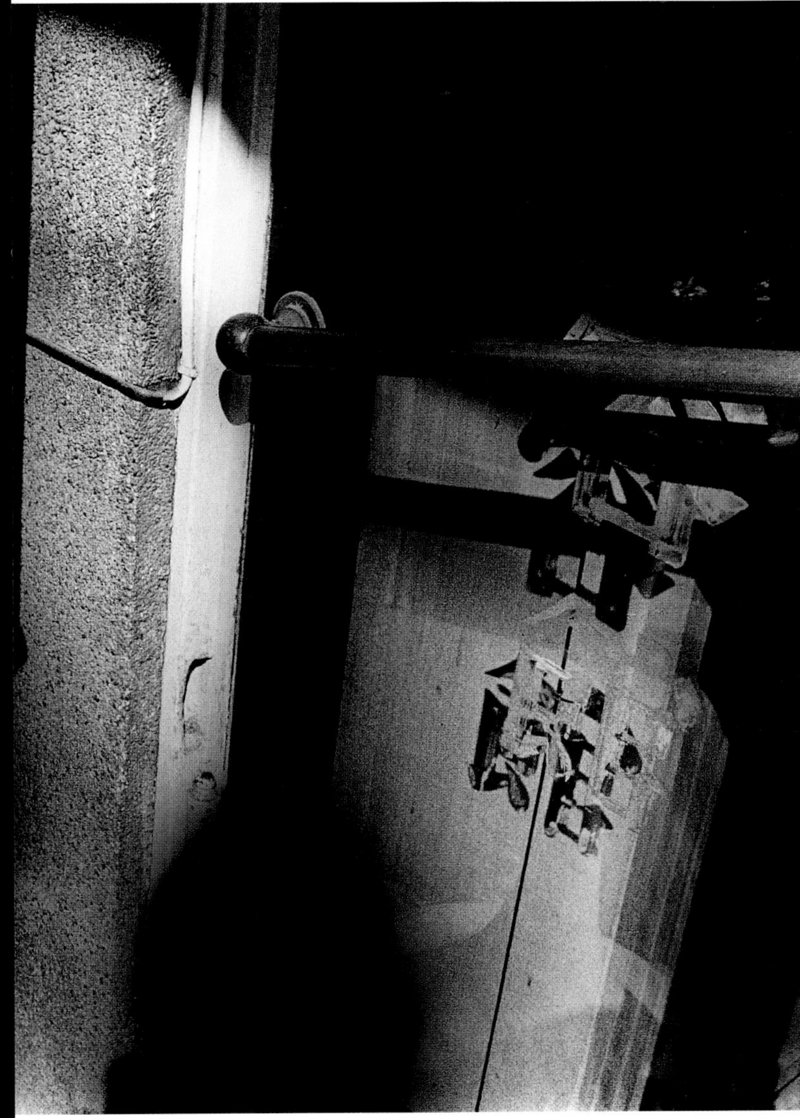

**(previous page) Barber's Shop, Miyagi, Japan, 1980.** Studios of sorts, in which appearances are contrived, barbers' shops have often interested photographers. Moriyama appears to have been attracted by the play of shadow from the latticed blind above, falling on the striped barber sign. The shadow of the dark door-handle establishes the angle of the light, but everything else in the picture must be more carefully assessed if the scene is to be grasped with any certainty. This invitation to fastidious scrutiny and appreciation is often extended to the viewer by photographers and might be seen as a form of scopophilia – a kind of visual eroticism.

**Peony, Kanagawa, Japan, 1980.** When European modernists photographed flowers and plants in the 1920s and 1930s they preferred compact examples: buds yet to unfurl and symmetrical seed-heads. The idea they wished to express was that Nature echoed our own careful engineering tendencies, offering an endorsement for our approaches. Moriyama's peony, on the other hand, is in full bloom, and perhaps even on the point of becoming overblown. In this respect, it might have symbolic undertones, hinting at the brevity of the creative moment. Moriyama had endured his own extended personal and creative crisis in the late 1970s.

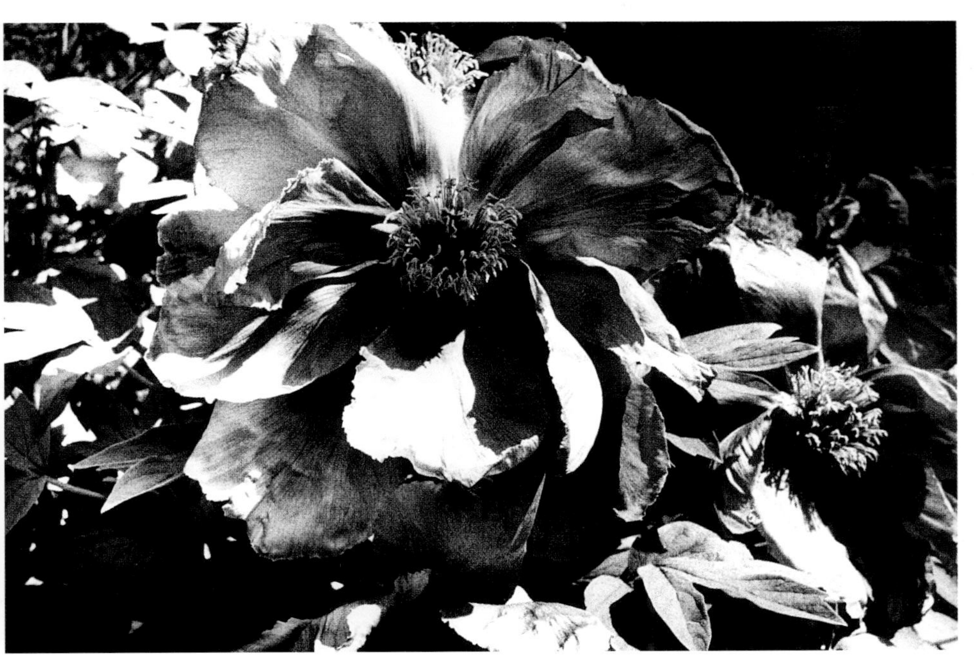

**Aeroplane, Kanagawa, Japan, 1981.** This appears to be an American bomber parked near the overgrown edge of a runway. The leading edge to the lower left allows us to orientate ourselves. The rope to the right is disconcertingly low tech, and introduces the kind of false note always attractive to Moriyama. Far from presenting the aeroplane in the conventional manner as an airborne whole, Moriyama offers as the bulk of the picture – its subject even – the riveting that holds the skin in place, and which can be thought of as a kind of contouring or mapping. As such, this is another testament to Moriyama's abiding commitment to the actual moment of perception.

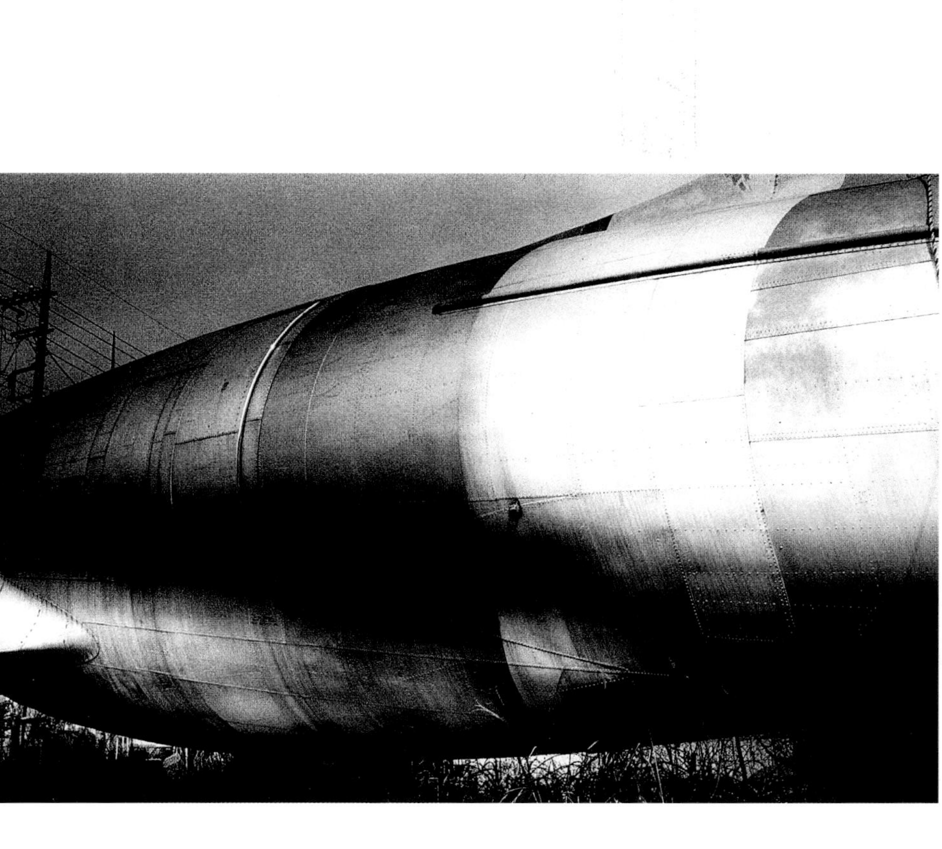

**Light and Shadow, Japan, 1981.** This picture was probably taken from the window of a suburban train bound for Tokyo. The iron girders and cement piers recall the heroic scenes of the industrialized nineteenth century. Principally, however, this is an intersection, a point on a map between termini. *Light and Shadow* is a traditional title in photography, perhaps the commonest of all. Moriyama's picture, however, is less a composition than a rendering of urban topography as a kind of sundial traversed by cast shadows, which complements the clock-time implicit in the railway system.

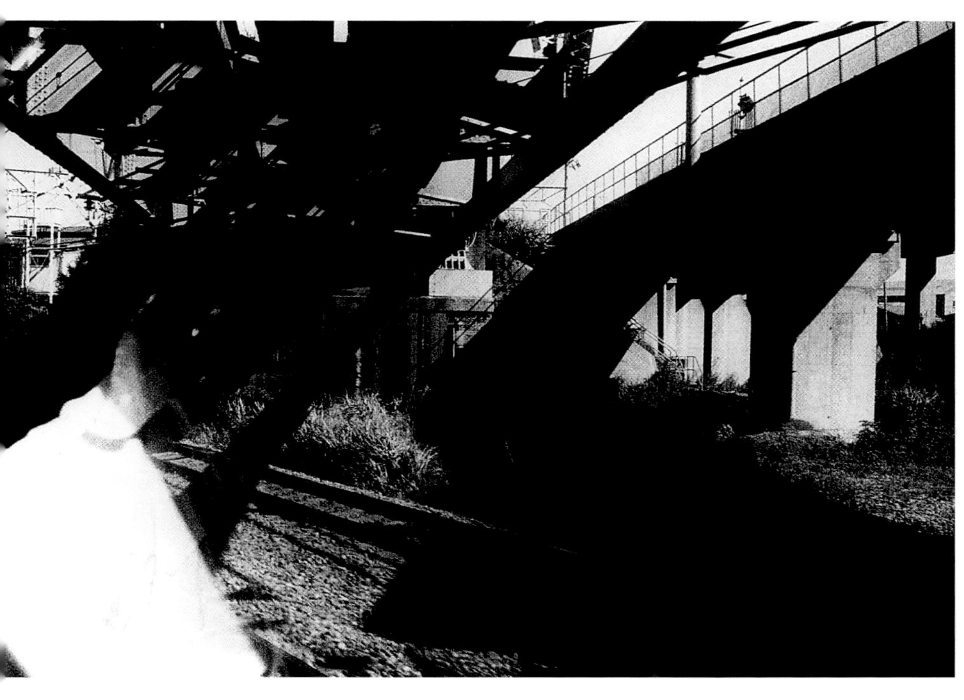

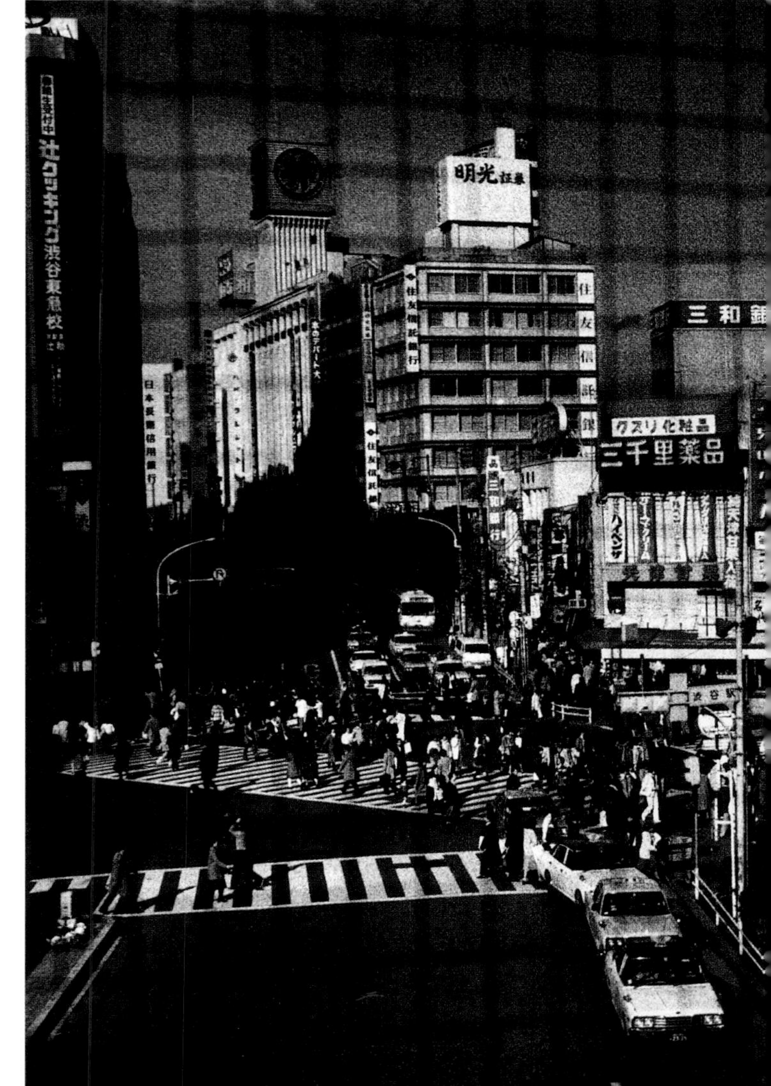
辻クッキング渋谷東急校
明光証券
住友信託銀行
日本長期信用銀行
クスリ化粧品
三千里薬品
渋谷駅

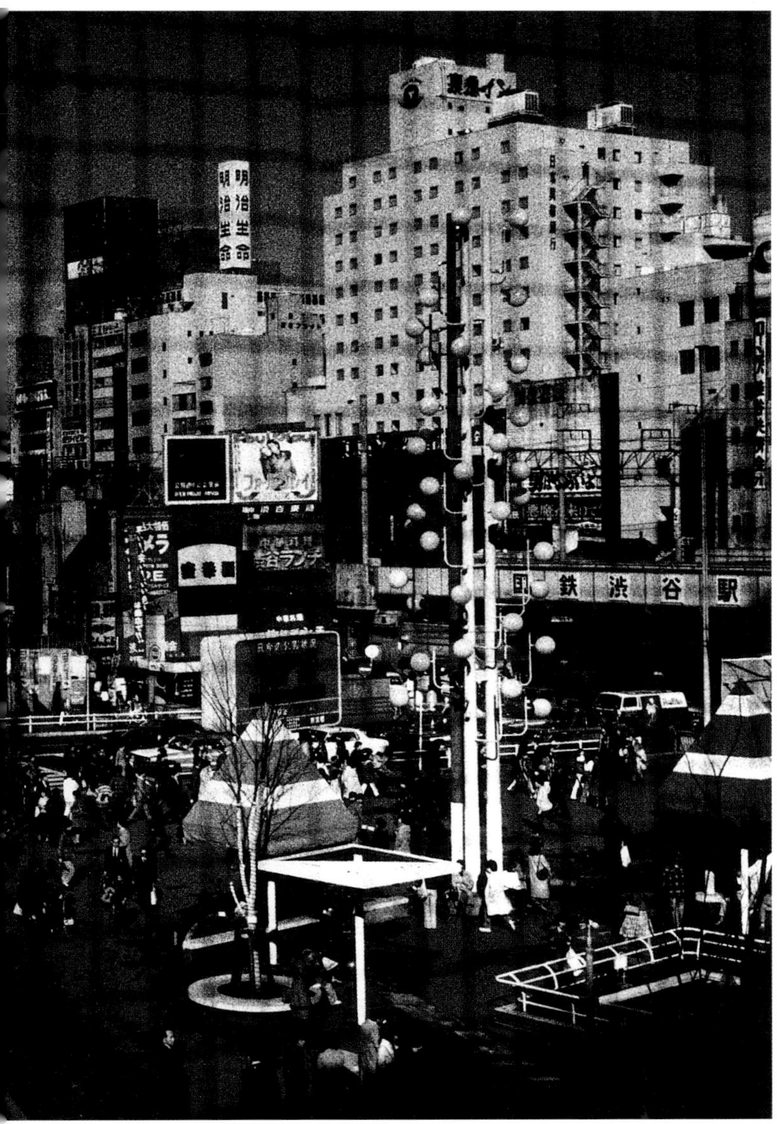
明治生命
明治生命
国鉄渋谷駅

**(previous page) Junction, Tokyo, Japan, 1981.** Faintly visible in the foreground of this bird's-eye view, taken from a building in front of Shibuya station, are the thin lines of steel wire embedded in the window-pane. This grid-like pattern gives the image the feel of an urban surveyor's photo. Postmodern aesthetics reject hierarchies, preferring to suggest that the world is made up of replaceable parts, all equally worthy of attention. Contemporary architecture, of the kind on show here, makes the same kind of suggestion. By extension, all social life can be understood as a continuum or system constituted of a myriad moving parts. Moriyama's matter-of-fact new topography presents such a view, including the city's inhabitants, who sprawl in front of Shibuya station.

**Bridge, Tokyo, Japan, 1981.** Although apparently a night scene, this picture of Hijiri Bridge near Ochanomizu station in Tokyo was in fact taken in broad daylight. On the negative, pedestrians can be seen crossing the bridge, but Moriyama burned out their forms in the darkroom. 'It feels to me that life is one continuous crossing of a never-ending bridge,' he said. He wanted this photograph to illustrate 'the junction between the spiritual and the mundane', as a kind of metaphysical image showing the 'crossing over from this shore to the other shore' that is a Buddhist metaphor for the crossing from *Samsara* (vanity) to *Nirvana* (enlightenment). The great strength of Japanese photography is due in part to its continuing access to such inherited wisdom and significance.

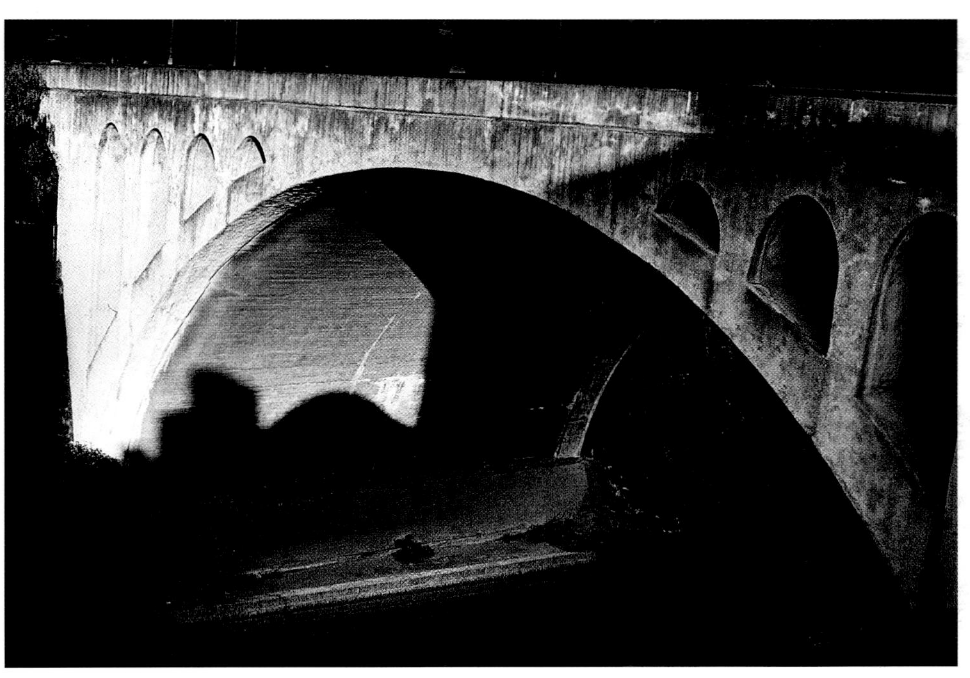

**Street, Tokyo, Japan, 1981.** Japanese boys used to have their hair shaved like this as a matter of ccurse. The formal and physical working out of pictures seems to have been of paramount importance and pleasure to Moriyama. The darkness of the hair intensifies towards the fretted profile of the head, complemented by the grooved and etched configurations in the foreground, like those of a map-maker or seismographer.

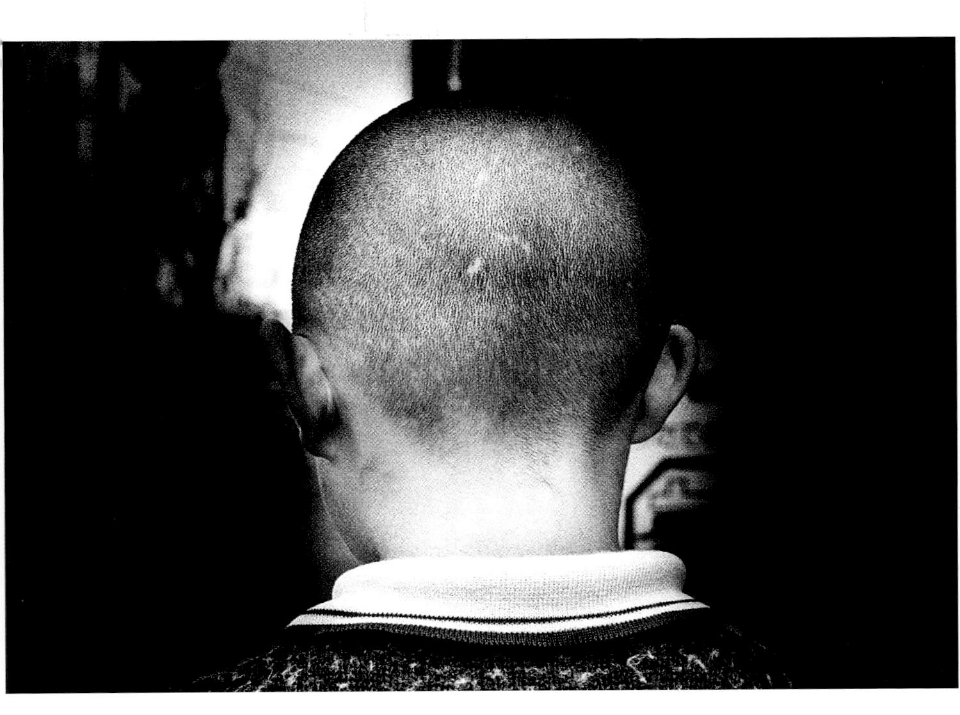

**Roadside, Aichi, Japan, 1981.** By excluding the tops of these dusty beer bottles, the photographer manages to keep us guessing for a while. This is as philosophical an image as that of the Hijiri bridge (page 101), for the bottles appear to form a series, emptying and ageing from the left, developing an almost geological or archaeological dimension before the series ends. They also resemble unexploded shells, dug out of long-forgotten battlefields. It is hard to resist the idea that Moriyama wants us to consider the trajectory of human life.

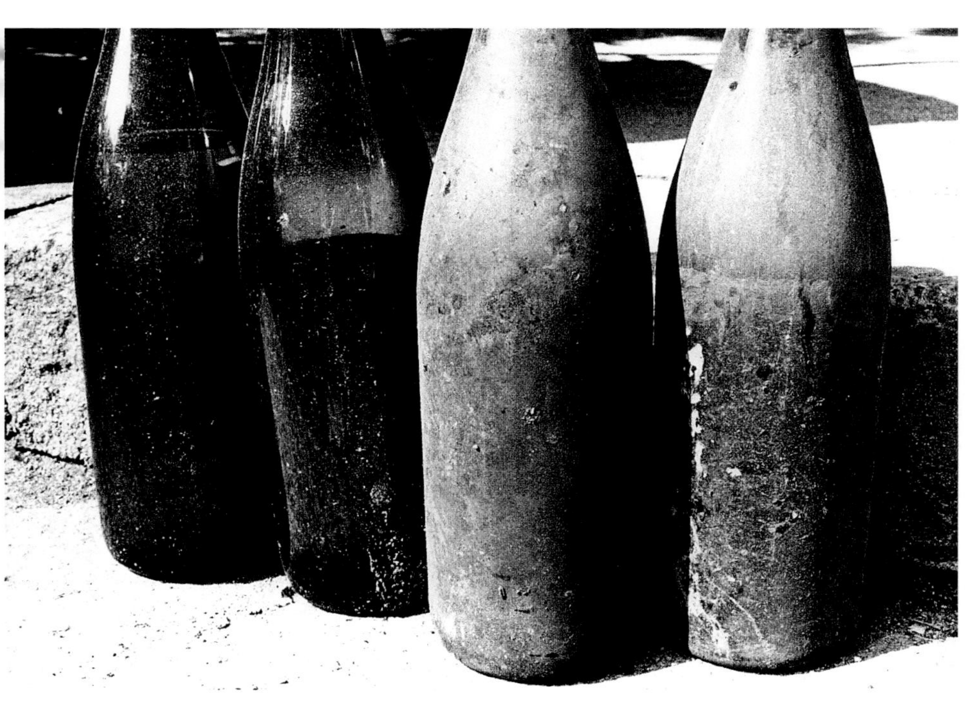

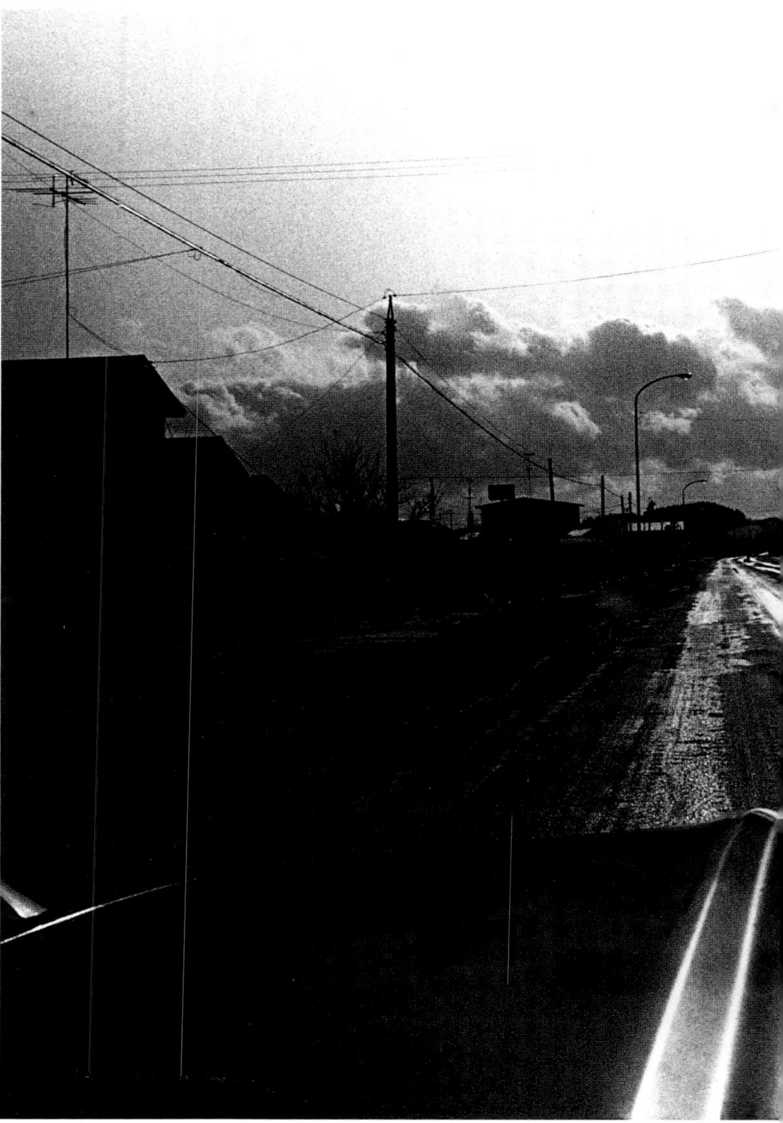

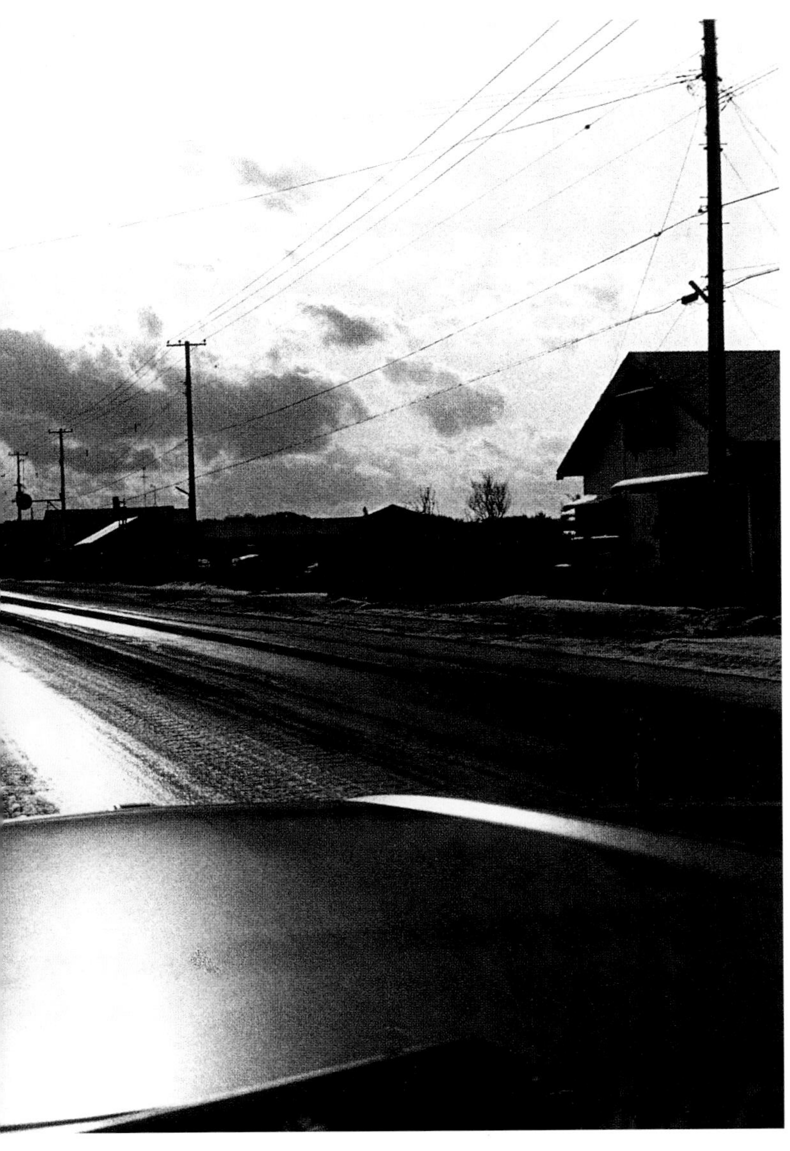

**(previous page) On the Road, Hokkaido, Japan, 1982.** The Japanese landscape is profusely punctuated by wires, which inevitably stand for the 'other' or elsewhere. In Moriyama's case, they represent the unsettled peripatetic lifestyle of the photographer. Where a classical landscapist might have wanted to see Hokkaido for itself, Moriyama insists that it should be seen from a certain point of view. One might call him, in the strictest sense, a phenomenologist.

**Town of Memory, Osaka, Japan, 1982.** This image came about through a visit paid by Moriyama to the city of Ikeda, Osaka, his birthplace. The bleached tone of the photograph evokes vague memories of childhood – Moriyama's was disturbed by the war and many relocations during the 1940s. The image looks almost like a negative augmented by desultory overdrawings. It is as if he were trying to develop his memory in the same way that he would develop a photograph.

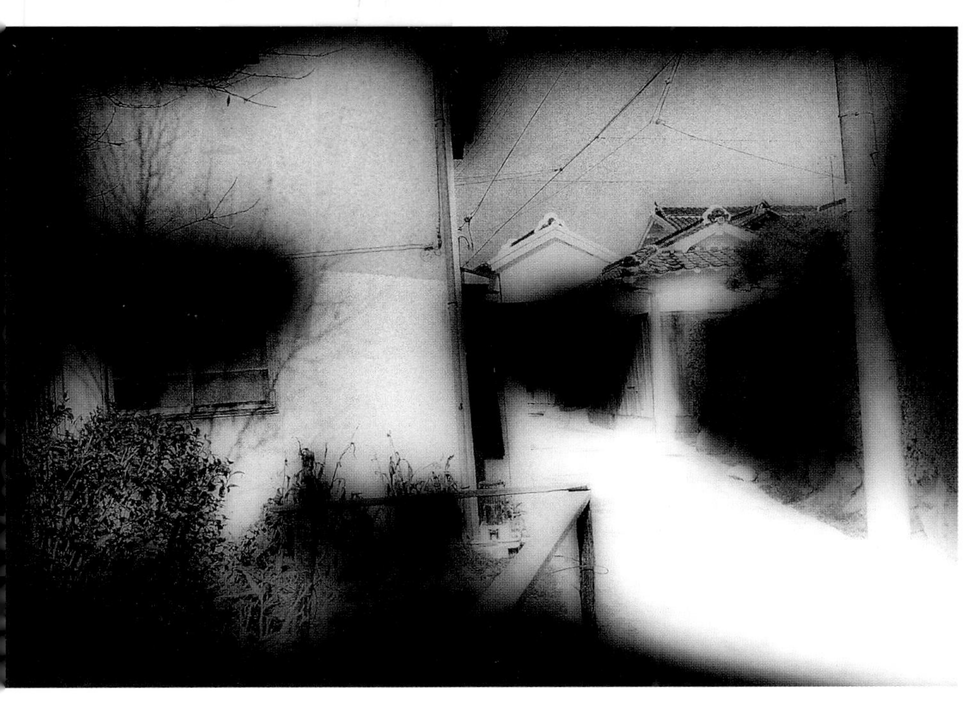

**Tights, Tokyo, Japan, 1986.** This picture was taken for the monthly journal *Shashin Jidai*, in which Moriyama kept a serial going for nine years, from the magazine's outset until it folded in 1989. *Shashin Jidai* supported him in the late 1980s, both financially and spiritually. Once one has got over the initial surprise of the structure – compressed thighs and calves – one begins to ask how the picture was arranged and lit, and to wonder empathetically about the placing and pressure of limb on limb. Figure photography has often invited such imaginary physical re-enactment.

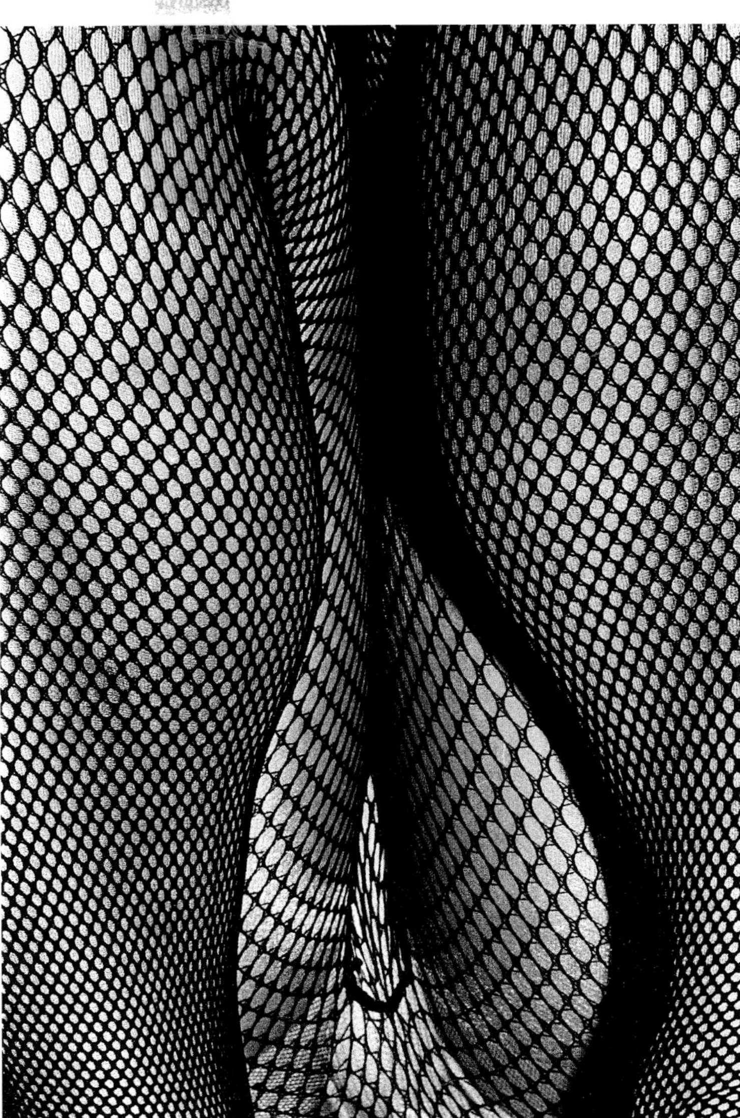

**Tiles, Fukushima, 1986.** This intriguing picture, also from the monthly *Shashin Jidai*, is a cropped view of bathroom tiles in a 'love hotel'. Though it resembles a homage to Op art, the works of that movement did not invite this kind of close, practical attention. What look at first sight like circular motifs begin to turn into hexagons low down on the wall; and on the step itself there are odd clusterings, as if the installer had lost his sense of rhythm from time to time. There can be no such thing, this work suggests, as a modular scheme perfectly realized.

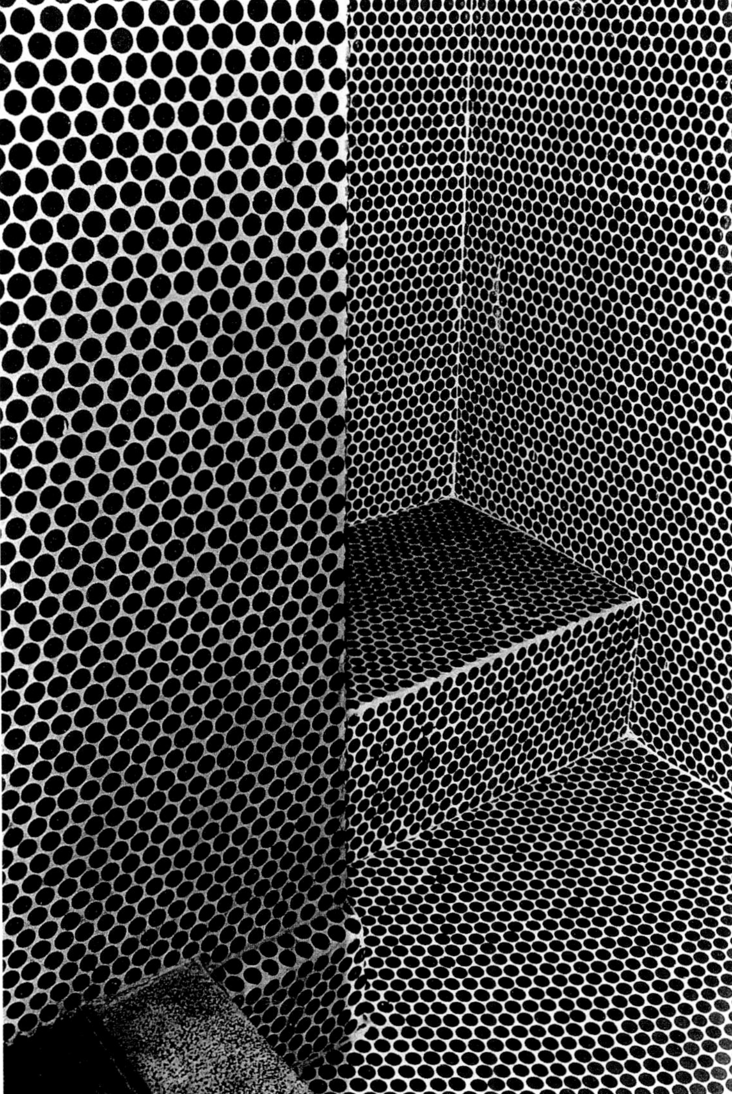

**Paris, France, 1989.** Moriyama began to tire of Tokyo and took a flat in Paris on the rue Mouffetard, in the fifth arrondissement. He went there several times during the year and began preparations for a book, *Tale of Two Cities: Paris/Tokyo*. A giant whale, airborne over the rooftops of Paris, must have been irresistible; photography, especially in France with its Surrealist traditions, has always been avid for such marvels.

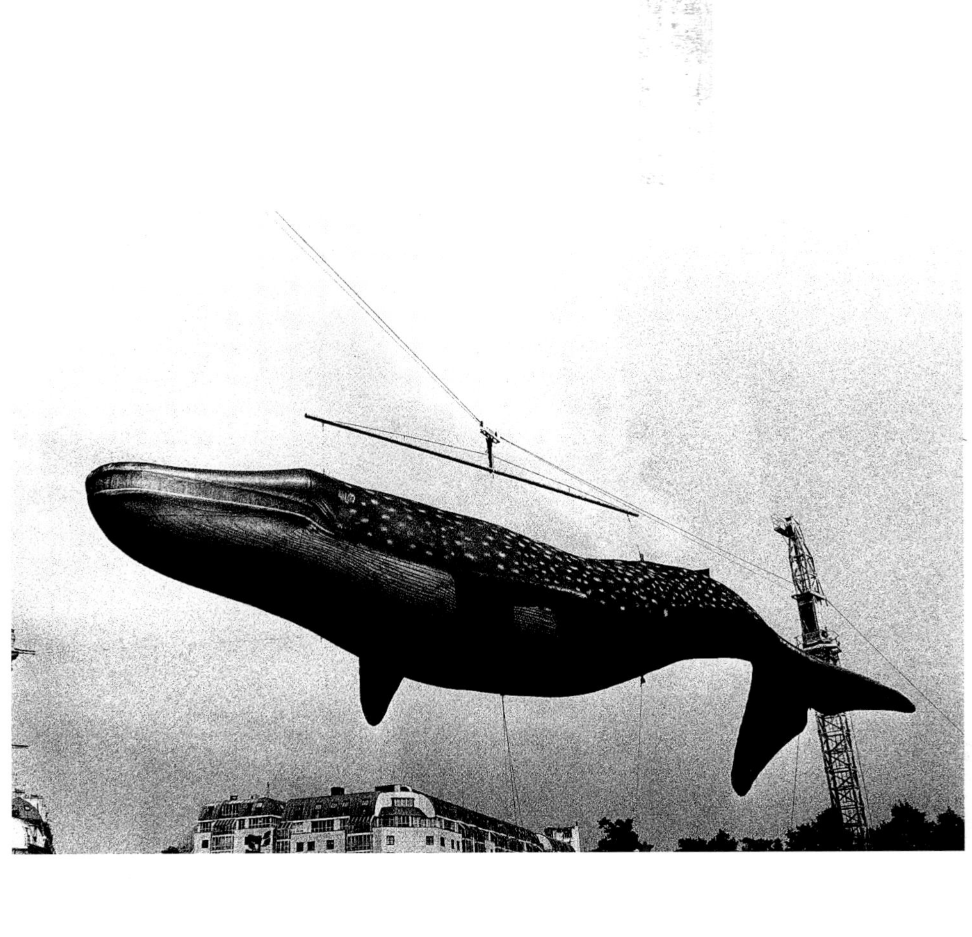

**Picture Tube, Kanagawa, Japan, 1991.** This image of a break in transmission was probably taken during one of Moriyama's infrequent visits to his wife and daughters, since his own home lacks a television set. It is interesting that an artist so accepting of the media should be without a TV, but it must be remembered that Moriyama's tendency has always been to read screened and printed images as if they were real surfaces in a tangible world. His whole career, in fact, has been devoted to refuting the idea of transparency and the fictions of re-presentation.

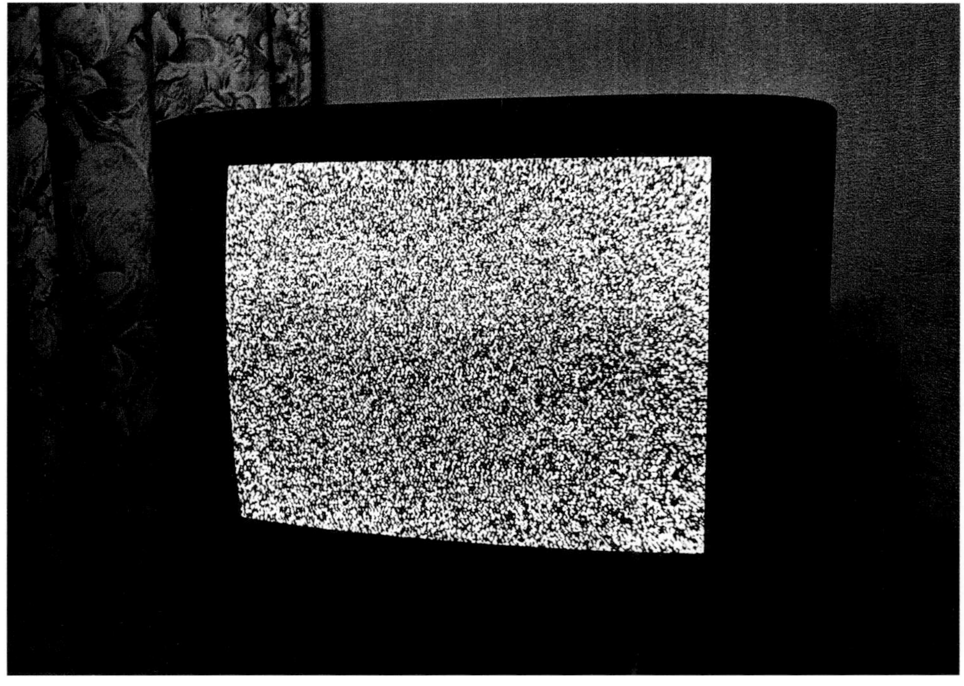

**Wax, Tokyo, Japan, 1992.** The clothing company Hysteric Glamour published a series of photographic books to assist their fashion merchandizing, one of which was devoted to new work by Moriyama. He spent an entire year 'stroll-shooting', and printed up a huge number of plates, eventually breaking his camera through overuse. The commission resulted in *Tokyo: Daido Hysteric*, nos. 4 & 6, published in 1993 and 1994 respectively, and in *Osaka: Daido Hysteric, no. 8*, 1997. Here, the waxer has inscribed what might be taken for a turbulent weather map on the Nissan's surface. Moriyama, as the rivet-heads in his aeroplane picture declare (page 95), has little time for bland, conceptual surfaces.

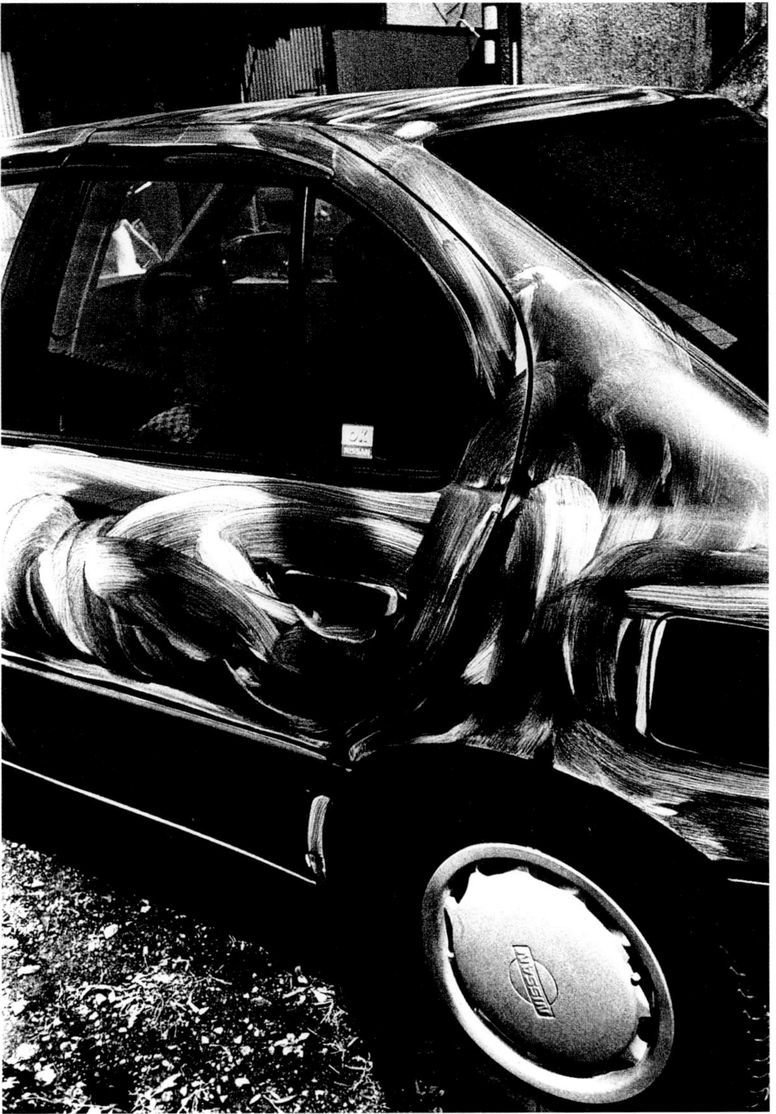
NISSAN

**Slum, Tokyo, Japan, 1992.** This image was taken in a narrow alleyway, looking upwards. Backstreet Japan is festooned with wires, pipes and ducts, and post-modern futurists, preoccupied by overcrowding and urban dysfunctionality, have often been attracted to environments of this sort. Moriyama's is an unusually radical view of the disappearing sky.

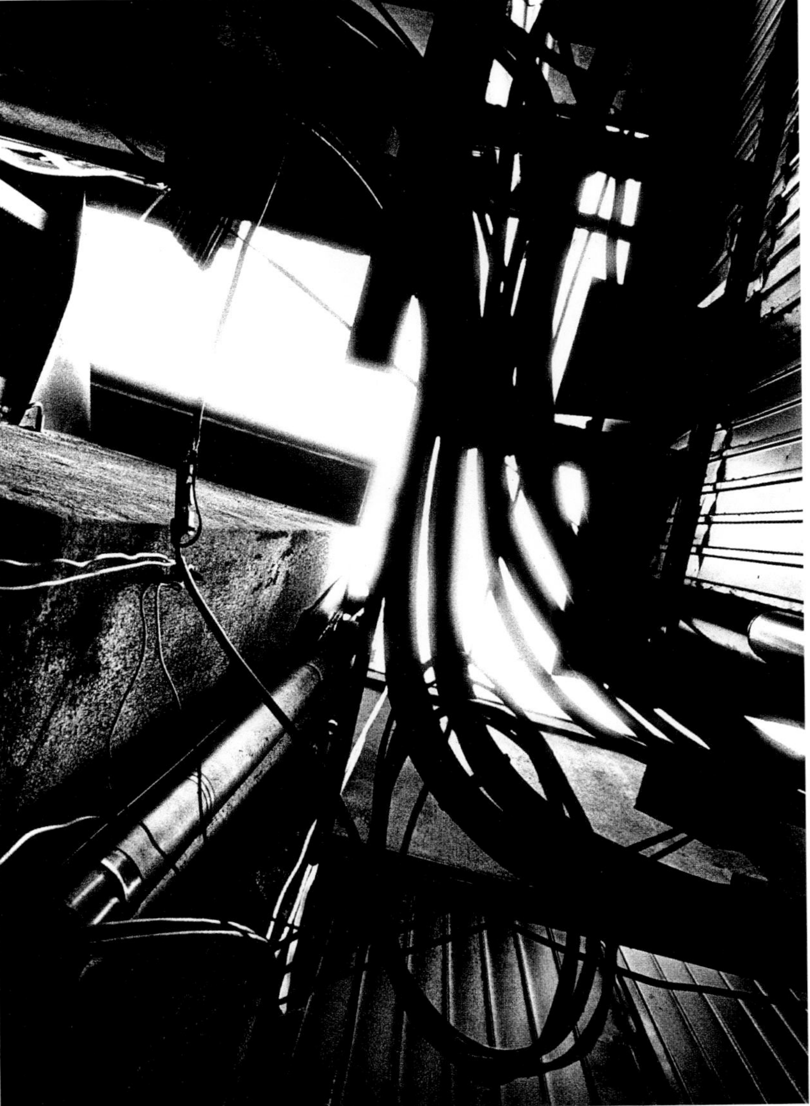

**Pavement, Tokyo, Japan, 1994.** Unlike volume one, the second volume of *Daido Hysteric* includes human figures in each image. Presumably this woman saw no alternative means of relief, despite the onrushing traffic. At least it was a drainage inlet – what, in an emergency, could be more sensible? However, it must also have been a test of nerve. The difference between this and average reportage is that Moriyama puts us too on the spot – even if only in our imaginations.

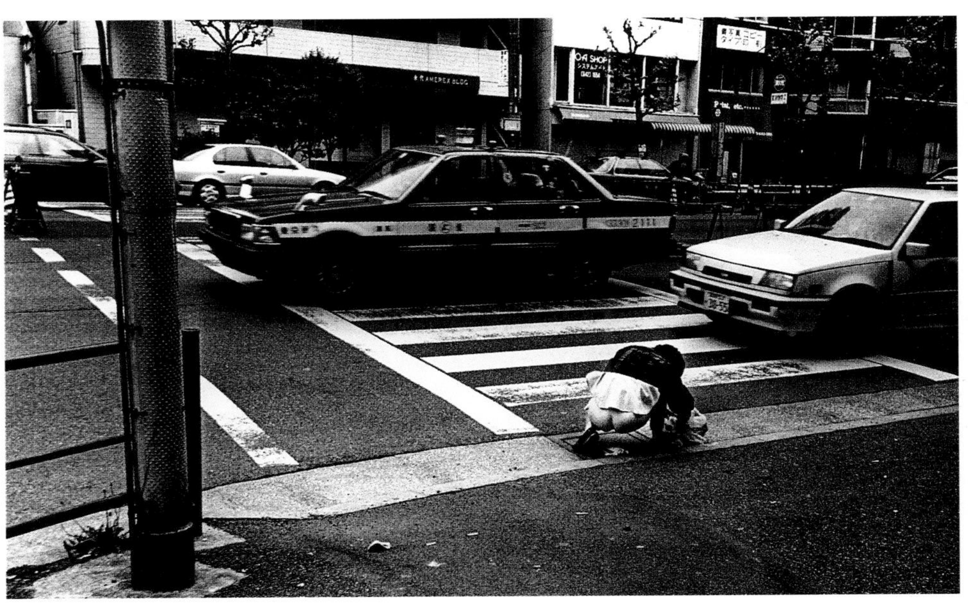
AMEREX BLDG
SHOP
システム
コピー

**1938** Born 10 October in Ikeda City, Osaka. Loses his twin brother, Kazumichi, aged one.

**1955–1958** Enrols in the design department of Osaka Municipal School of Industrial Art, and works as a graphic designer.

**1958** Father is killed in a train accident.

**1959–1961** Goes to work in the studio of Osaka-based photographer Takeji Iwamiya. Earns a living taking souvenir portrait pictures for passengers and sailors arriving at Kobe Pier.

**1961–1963** Moves to Tokyo. Tries to join VIVO, a prestigious photographer's group, only to find it has just disbanded. But Eikoh Hosoe, a member of VIVO, employs him as an assistant. Marries Michiko Sugiwara.

**1961** Becomes freelance photographer. Moves to Zushi, Kanagawa.

**1965** Publishes his photographs of US airbase, Yokosuka, in *Camera Mainichi*.

**1966** Publishes 'Showmen' series in *Camera Mainichi* and is awarded the Most Promising Photographer Award by the Japan Photo Critics Association.

**1967** Joins PROVOKE, an influential but short-lived photography group, at the invitation of Takuma Nakahira, one of its founders.

**1968** Publishes his first book, *Japan: A Photo Theatre*. Begins five-year association with the photographic magazine *Ashahi Camera*, which publishes his series 'Accident'.

**1970** Shoots nudes for *Playboy* magazine, designs adverts, and makes numerous TV and radio appearances. Exhibits 'Scandal', series of billboards covered in rephotographed magazine adverts. PROVOKE is dissolved.

**1971** Series 'Journey to Something', including many photographs which later become known as his most important work, is published in *Asahi Camera*. Makes a trip to New York.

**1972** Publishes two books of his photographs, *Farewell Photography* and *Hunter*. Starts magazine, *Records*, which he self-publishes.

**1974** Establishes school for photography, 'Workshop', with Shomei Tomatsu, Nobuyoshi Araki and others. First solo exhibition, 'The Tales of Tono'. His work is included in the exhibition 'New Japanese Photography', curated by Shoji Yamagishi and held at the Museum of Modern Art, New York.

**1975** Appointed full-time lecturer at Tokyo Vocational School of Photography.

**1976** His work is included in the exhibition, 'Fifteen Photographers Today', at the National Museum of Modern Art, Tokyo.

**1979** His work is included in 'Japan: A Self-Portrait', an exhibition held at ICP, New York, and curated by Shoji Yamagishi.

**1980–1985** Travels in Europe, visiting William Klein in Paris and holding a solo exhibition of his work in Graz, Austria. Publishes compilation of writings *Memories of a Dog* and *A Dialogue with Photography*.

**1987–1994** Opens private gallery called 'room 801'. Publishes photographic books *A Journey to Nakaji* (1987), *Moriyama Daido* 1970–1979 (1989), *Daido Hysteric, no. 4* (1993), *Moriyama Daido Colour* (1993) and *Daido Hysteric no. 6* (1994).

**1994–1998** Publishes writings *From Photography/To Photography* (1995), and numerous photographic books, including *Imitation* (1995), *Time of a Dog* (1995) and *Hunter-Replica* (1997).

**1999** Solo exhibition at San Francisco Museum of Modern Art, which then travels worldwide and is accompanied by exhibition catalogue, *Daido Moriyama: Stray Dog*. Also publishes photographic books *Moriyama Daido Colour 2*, *Water Dream* and *Passage 4*.

Photography is the visual medium of the modern world. As a means of recording, and as an art form in its own right, it pervades our lives and shapes our perceptions.

**55** is a new series of beautifully produced, pocket-sized books that acknowledge and celebrate all styles and all aspects of photography.

Just as Penguin books found a new market for fiction in the 1930s, so, at the start of a new century, Phaidon **55**s, accessible to everyone, will reach a new, visually aware contemporary audience. Each volume of 128 pages focuses on the life's work of an individual master and contains an informative introduction and 55 key works accompanied by extended captions.

As part of an ongoing program, each **55** offers a story of modern life.

**Daido Moriyama** (b.1938) has made a radical and innovative impact on the photographic world. His snapshot aesthetic and no-viewfinder style have succeeded in challenging the medium's prevailing orthodoxies. As a founder member of *PROVOKE* magazine, and as a lecturer and theorist, he has been a formative influence on the new generation of Japanese photographers.

**Kazuo Nishii** is a film and photography critic. He was Editor-in-Chief of the Japanese photography magazine *Camera Mainichi* from 1983 to 1985, and has written several books, including *Why Still 'Provoke' Now?* (1996).

Phaidon Press Limited
Regent's Wharf
All Saints Street
London N1 9PA

Phaidon Press Inc.
180 Varick Street
New York NY 10014

www.phaidon.com

First published 2001

ISBN 0 7148 4023 8

Designed by Julia Hasting
Printed in Hong Kong

A CIP record of this book is available from the British Library.